POCKET GUIDE TO LONG TERM CARE FOR NURSING

By: **D. A. Terry Anderson, RN, BSN**

POCKET GUIDE TO LONG TERM CARE NURSING FOR NURSING

Cover designed by Molly M. Camacho

TABLE OF CONTENTS

PREFACE

I am so excited to present this book to the many folks who care for the sick in the Long-Term Care/Short-Term Rehab (LTC/STR) settings. Prior to working in this area of nursing, my experience was in Acute Care, I then transitioned to; LTC/STR center. The two health care settings contrasted greatly; I was astonished at how the two worlds of caring for patients were so different. Let me explain; staffing ratios are less in Acute Care, while in the LTC/STR facility the nurse-to-patient ratio is greater, that was difficult for me to grasp. I personally felt that continuing education was mostly centered around what was mandatory and required; and it was rare to find funding available for additional training. In contrast the Acute Care setting always had additional continuing education made available for staff members. The required education for each setting was different depending on the nursing role. I tried very hard to understand the reason for the difference.

Out of my experience came this resource which will be valuable to anyone desiring to work in this arena or to pursue aspirations of a leadership role. This passion drove me to create this pocket guide to help others understand the setting. A reference such as this pocket guide would have made my experience much smoother at first. I have made it a lifelong goal to make this pocket guide available to others who are hoping to gain more knowledge and to help them advance in their career. This pocket guide is meant to give an overview of the job roles and specific functions in the LTC/STR environment. With this pocket guide in hand a prospective Supervisor, a new Assistant Director of Nursing (ADON), Infection Preventionist Nurse (IPN), a Staff Development Coordinator (SDC) or a supervisor, will be able to perform their roles with greater confidence. This is an overview for a nursing student becoming a Registered Nurse (RN), or an Licensed Vocational Nurse/Licensed Practical Nurse

(LVP/LPN); and a Certified Nursing Assistant (CNA) whose goal is to work in this healthcare environment.

My life's work has been accomplished, my desire to make a difference for years to come, assisting healthcare workers that desire to understand the daily operation in a LTC/STR facility. This information is intended to serve as a helpful guide and is NOT ALL inclusive of all methods, practices, and theories for helping to train staff, as there are many valuable tools available. Many successes to those who will read this.

ACKNOWLEDGEMENT

I would like to celebrate all the wonderful individuals who supported me through this journey. First, I would like to salute all healthcare workers who work in the LTC/STR setting they are my heroes. It takes a special kind of person to commit to this area of healthcare, Mitch Romero, Physical Therapist (PT) so rightfully expresses that caring for patients is a calling, so much more than a profession. Special thanks to Deveney Tucker, RN, BSN for her endless editing, to Lilli Palin, RN for her timely advice, my family for continued support and encouraging me all the way through and Fawny Vernon, M.Ed., for her comprehensive editing. Gina, Celeste, Sheryl, Romney, Ruth, Stephen, Karen, and Sarah they prayed for me and were the fuel that kept me energized; you all assisted in sustaining me. I thank God for you all.

ORGANIZATION

Each chapter is provided with (1) A learning objective
and (2) A discussion of the topic

CHAPTER ONE

The History of the Nursing Home, OBRA 1987

Learning Objectives

The beginning of this book begins with the history of the Long-Term Care industry and how the industry arrived at its status today. The industry was never monitored as much in the past as it is today.

The Nursing Home Industry was transformed by the Nursing Home Reform Act (NHRA) of 1987. Prior to this historic event, the Institute of Medicine (IOM) performed a study in the 1980s on how care could be improved. Recommendations were then submitted to the federal government resulting in the Omnibus Reconciliation Act (OBRA) of 1987. This landmark enactment goal was to improve the quality of care in nursing homes, impacting care on all fronts (IOM, 2001).

After this law was passed, many rights and privileges that were previously denied, were now mandated. The new laws enhanced delivery of care which protected patients from abuse and allowed everyone to voice complaints and have concerns addressed without retaliation. The law also gave patients the opportunity to choose their own physician and pharmacy, and in addition the right to have special accommodations and to have all needs met in a timely manner and allow visitation privileges. The NHRA changed practices that required a thorough assessment of each resident with a status completed on admission to the center and to develop an individualized care plan after gathering the data. Prevention of abuse became paramount, strictly scrutinized making each allegation of abuse a reportable offence to the Department of Public Health (DPH). The new law mandated that each nursing home employ a Director of Nursing (DON) and a Licensed Nursing Home Administrator (LNHA) to oversee the daily operations. Physical Rehabilitation Therapy is required to be provided to each patient to maximize their optimal level of function requiring coordination with physical, occupational and speech therapy, as well as, medical and nursing care for each resident. Another significant result of the Reform Act was a requirement that family members were to be notified of changes that occur with the patient such as: medication changes, any new orders or interventions, changes in clinical condition and the need for transfer to an acute care setting (CMS Manual System, 2004).

Similarly impacting was the requirement for the certification of nursing assistants. In 1990 the Senate discussed the 1987 OBRA changes to the nursing home landscape including how training for nursing assistants would be funded. States were now compelled to have all nursing assistants trained and certified for their positions prior to hiring. In the past, training was not a requirement to secure a nursing assistant job in the Long-Term Care (LTC) setting. Since then each nursing assistant has had to obtain certification and provide proof of training including any documentation of continuing education training (Senate, 1990). Documentation of all credentials and training must be filed for each new certified nursing staff to the Department of Public Health (DPH). Other significant changes to LTC included maintaining individual bank accounts for each patient, allowing patients to have access to their own medical records and acceptance of patients with mental illness. Additional improvements involved the certification for the admission of Medicaid or Medicare patients and preventing centers from securing private payments from family members of Non-Medicare or Non-Medicaid covered items (Hollis, nd). Changes in the law also affected patient's visitation rights. Visitors are now allowed at whatever time they desire while maintaining privacy at the same time. Health inspection results are to be made available for display and on demand. Patients are able exercise rights to choose whether to move from one room to another.

A resident is allowed to bring in personal items to the center and request reasonable accommodations to the capacity allotted in the space where they reside (State Operations Manual, 2016). The face of the nursing home continues to change with new regulations and standards to improve the quality of care on a regular basis.

Resources

CMS Manual System, (2004), Retrieved from:
https://www.cms.gov/Regulations-and-Guidance/Guidance/Transmittals/downloads/R5SOM.pdf

Hollis, (nd), Federal nursing home reform act from the omnibus budget reconciliation act of 1987. Retrieved from:http://www.ncmust.com/doclib/OBRA87 summary.pdf

Institute of Medicine, (2001), Improving the quality of care in long term care, shaping the future of health. Retrieved from: https://pdfs.semanticscholar.org/e494/ac95ffc dbf96f95d91a80579977f3d40fd30.pdf

Senate, (1990), Congressional Record, Senate Enhanced State Medicaid matching funds extension for training nurses' aides pursuant to OBRA 1987. Retrieved from: https://www.gpo.gov/fdsys/search/search.acti on?na= publishdatehier&se= 1990false&sm=

&flr=&ercode=&dateBrowse=&govAuthBrowse
=&collection=&historical=false&st=obra+1987
&psh=&sbh=&tfh=&originalSearch=obra+1987
&fromState=&sb=re&ps=10&sb=re&ps=10

State Operations Manual, (2016). Retrieved from: http://www.hpm.umn.edu/nhregsplus/Resour ces%20and%20Publications/CMS_Survey_Re sources/CMS/Appx_SOM_483.30%20-%20Nursing%20Services.pdf

CHAPTER TWO

Culture Change

Learning Objectives

This section on culture change will detail the transformation in the nursing home industry. Maintaining dignity in the nursing home by making the atmosphere home like and treating residents respectfully while providing necessary care at all times.

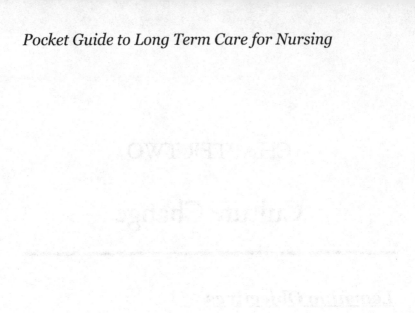

Culture Change

The Nursing Home Act of 1987 permanently disrupted the process of how Nursing Homes were run. One of the changes that resulted from that enactment was Culture Change. Shield et al, (2014) mentions reasons behind the turnaround in the Nursing Home industry. Culture change transformed from an institutionally driven form of operation to a person-centered type of care. The focus of the change included emphasis on "choice, dignity, respect, self-determination and purposeful living" (Texas Long Term Care Institute, 2011). Culture change has been positive in affecting the daily operations in ways that promote a home like atmosphere.

Modifications included decreasing center noise from overhead announcement pages on the premise that no one would normally install a public address system in their home to make announcements that disturb their entire household. Overhead pages are kept to a minimum and are reserved for emergencies. One other distinct change for centers were the names assigned to nursing units, names given before were more institutional and recommendations. for naming units today are more personal. Preferred names could be that of a street name or names of a plant or a shrub. The same home like atmosphere is applied to the patient's rooms with personalized items that reflect their preferences in decorating. The most impacting adjustment in culture change was also revamping of the dining atmosphere. Previously, food carts with food trays were transported to the nursing floors, then delivered to each room. Delayed delivery would result in lukewarm or cold meals and patient's subsequent complaint.

To improve on the dining experience, many centers introduced "Fine Dining" with a formal like dining experience or meals provided on steam tray tables. The meals are served hot directly on each unit for those who are unable to appear to the dining room because of their medical limitation or preference not to attend and choose to eat in their rooms. Dining and steam tray tables allow patients to choose from food options offered on a menu with considerations for each patient's diet. The designated dining area in the center is arranged and decorated to have the experience of a restaurant style atmosphere. Ambulatory and non-ambulatory patients are assisted to the dining area and served like a community restaurant.

A nurse or CNA must be present to assist with meals and verify the appropriate diet is served and to observe for any safety needs. Culture change also emphasized maintaining patient dignity while in the dining experience. All needs must be met while in the dining area especially toileting needs. Staff members are to avoid referring to the patients with names like "honey" or "sweetie". Bibs also preferably called clothing protectors are offered to patients and each person is given the opportunity to choose to wear one at meal times or choose not to. A patient's appearance throughout the day should be appropriately dressed, clothes neat and clean, hair trimmed and brushed and with no offensive odors or obvious stains to clothing. Foley catheter bags are covered for privacy at all times in and out of the center. Patients should always be up and out of bed unless there are specific Physician orders for bed rest and consistently provide meaningful and stimulating activities both individually and corporately.

Culture Change is a work in progress and continues to improve the patient experience since its inception. During the facility inspection period a surveyor will observe activities on all shifts, to determine whether patient needs are being met in a timely manner; the surveyors will observe for culture change enhancements and note whether the patient is always the focus of care.

Resources

Shield, R. R., Looze, J., Tyler, D., Lepore, M., & Miller, S. C. (2014). Why and How Do Nursing Homes Implement Culture Change Practices? Insights from Qualitative Interviews in a Mixed Methods Study. *Journal of Applied Gerontology: The Official Journal of the Southern Gerontological Society, 33*(6), 737–763. http://doi.org/10.1177/0733464813491141

Texas Long Term Care Institute, (2011) Culture Chang in Long Term Care: It's History and Development, Principles, Implementation and Legislation. Retrieved from: digital.library.txstate.edu.

CHAPTER THREE

Roles in the Daily Functions of the Center

<u>Learning objectives</u>

There are several important roles in the function of a center and this section will elaborate on the duties and functions for successful daily operations.

Center Roles and Duties

Center roles have the responsibility for ensuring daily functions in a center are carried out efficiently by addressing complaints, investigating and completing incident reports in a timely manner. Conducting various meetings and monitoring patients for protection and safety consistently in survey readiness. The DON and Administrator collaborates with their teams for the overall operation of the center in all areas of function. Attentiveness to the flow of all processes, meals, nursing care, environmental concerns, supplies, rehabilitation, recreation, services provided and nursing rounds. Monitoring of interventions to prevent pressure ulcers, prevention of the spread of infection. Processes for survey preparation, culture change, dining, cleanliness of the center, appropriate looking appearances of each patient, Staff growth and development through education, discipline, employee development and consistent recruiting through interviews, as well as addressing scheduling issues and staffing needs.

The Center License Home Administrator

The Center Administrator is a Licensed Home Administrator (LHA), who directs and oversees the operation of a LTC Center and may report to a corporate entity or Board of Directors. The LHA manages these departments according to regulations from the State Operations Manual (SOM) and the standards set by the Center for Medicare Services (CMS). The LHA's role may comprise of the following; budgeting, staffing, and day to day operations in all departments. All departments report to the LHA who is kept abreast of problems, concerns, and issues on all levels, with constant communication on center issues as is primary in order for department heads to efficiently operate and direct their staff. The LHA is responsible for securing physician and other medical contractors desiring to provide services in the center. The task of operating a center regulated by the state and CMS is very daunting but carefully following the SOM and with a committed team the LHA will guide the processes with confidence. Departments directly under the LHA are Nursing, Rehabilitation Therapy, Housekeeping, Laundry, Dietary, Maintenance, Business Office, Administration, Recreation, Social Services Admissions, Marketing, and Human Resources.

Director of Nursing

The job of a Director of Nursing DON can be a rewarding position and at the same time challenging. The responsibility of leading a team of staff members into achieving center goals requires tenacity, discipline, knowledge, and vision. The DON reports to the LHA and is responsible for the nursing services, encompassing full patient centered care. This includes the management of staffing, ensuring proper delivery of care and services, and maintaining a high level of care throughout all shifts. This is accomplished through trained, competent, and committed nursing staff. They are responsible for overseeing the training, competencies and closely monitoring all aspects of patient care. The DON works parallel with the center LHA to achieve these goals. This leadership role requires a team approach that is present and in agreement with company facility goals and expectations. This team includes the Assistant Director of Nursing (ADON), Staff Development Coordinator (SDC), Infection Preventionist Nurse (IPN), Nursing Supervisor, Charge Nurses and Certified Nursing Assistants (CNA). Other clinical roles include Physicians, Physician's Assistant (PA), Nurse Practitioners (NP), Registered Dietician (RD), and personnel in the Physical Rehabilitation Department.

Assistant Director of Nursing

The Assistant Director of Nursing (ADON) supports the DON in whatever capacity is necessary for the effective functioning of the center. Some centers combine roles such as ADON and Wound Care Nurse (WCN), ADON and SDC or Infection Prevention Nurse (IPN), and Staff Development Coordinator (SDC) depending upon the center size and capacity needs. The collaborative effort from the DON and ADON helps increase the centers efficiency. In the absence of the DON and the center LHA, the ADON functions as the point person center representative.

Admissions, Business Office, and Insurance Roles

The office of Admissions, Business Office, and Insurance responsibilities are sometimes combined in a center. The Admissions Office is the gatekeeper for new admissions arriving to the center. Centers generally establish a relationship with different acute care hospitals who refer potential patients preparing for discharge to a lower level of care. Multiple centers may receive the same patient referral and whichever center can provide the care needed and accepts the potential patient is awarded the referral. Family members play a decisive role and may choose a center that is near their residing location. If there is no family involvement, then the Nurse Case Manager or Social Worker will make the best decision for the patient's needs.

These referrals are generally sent out throughout the day, and therefore, the center should always be prepared to receive a new admission. When accepting new patients, the facility must assure they are equipped with necessary medical equipment and trained staff capable of providing the needed care for the new patient arriving. The Admissions Department in the center informs the DON/ADON, or the nursing supervisor of the patient's potential arrival and any special equipment or supplies that are essential for their nursing stay. A patient may require orders for a Negative Pressure Wound Vacuum (NPWV) or necessitate a G-tube with a special kind of tube feeding. The center must be prepared since failing to provide the necessary services needed would cause a non-compliance in care. Coordination for each new admission includes the following: housekeeping who organizes cleaning and preparing the patient's room, while the nursing staff ensures all items necessary for the patient's care is available. The Admissions Department is responsible for obtaining the following information at intake: the patient's basic information, legal name, or alias, if necessary, date of birth, social security number, code status, next of kin, family member or power of attorney, insurance information, any allergies (if known) and including preferences. Upon admission, each patient is assigned a physician from the pool of center physicians based on availability or physician coverage assigned on any day of the week. Once entered into the Electronic Health Record (EHR) each patient is assigned a Medical Record Number (MRN) and verified by the Business Office. The patient record is accessible by all departments at the center, as necessary for care, however, prudence should be taken to prevent duplication of records since there could be a cost to rectify the duplication, as well as being problematic with errors for billing.

The Business Office is responsible for the accounts payable and receivables within the center. If in a small center, the department may be assigned the center staff's payroll or have it outsourced to a third party if there is no corporate payroll department. Resident trust fund accounts are also assigned to the Business Office with patient's accounts being held in individual bank accounts. Patients may withdraw from their accounts during the banking hours set by the center and arrangements are made to make funds available during off hours. This department also reports on the daily census including new admission, discharges, transfers, as well as, any patient who deceased in the previous 24 hours. The census is critical for reporting and billing with Medicare, therefore; it must be verified by performing a physical count of all the patients present and confirm any discharges or admissions that occurred within a 24-hour period. Information is verified for each patient room and provided to the Business Office for billing purposes.

The insurance liaison confirms the payer source for each admission and obtains authorization, provides clinical data, requests extended stay and provides proof for the level of stay. This liaison's individual role consistently communicates with the insurance companies, nursing, physicians, rehabilitation therapy and the Minimum Data Set (MDS) team for continued care success.

Social Services

The Social Service Department operates as the in-house patient advocate and works to ensure all patients receive necessary services available. The Social Services Department is heavily involved with an admission throughout the patient's stay and through the discharge process back to the community or other level of care. Based on the size of a center, two Social Service professionals may be employed, one serves as a director and the other as an assistant. This department investigates complaints in every situation and prevents abuse and assures necessary services will transition through discharge. Payer sources vary in the LTC facility; however, most patients are covered by either Medicare, Medicaid, or other forms of insurance. Individual patients without payer resources are assisted to obtain essential treatment, equipment, medications, and other needed medical services. According to Patrick & Freed (2012), at least 84 billion dollars was spent on LTC services for the elderly over a six-year period. The Social Service department informs and protects the rights of each patient. A prime example of this is a change of patient rooms. The Social Service Department ensures that all parties associated in the decision prior to the initial transfer is informed and that all parties agree to the transfer. Documentation is necessary to show communication involving all parties, so that the decision to relocate is solely left to the patient to be voluntary and without coercion. The Social Service personnel also play an essential role in the grieving process whenever a patient passes away.

The Social Service Department initiates services for hospice care, coordinates pastoral or chaplaincy care, counseling, and support for the grieving families. This department is integral to maintaining patient advocacy, securing needed services, and observing patients completely from admission to discharge.

Physician Coverage

Physician coverage in LTC centers has changed over time and may be provided by several physicians or other qualified medical staff. The Medical Director combined with several other physicians directly under him, provides the medical care for each patient. The enactment of the Affordable Care Act (ACA) increased the need for diligence in monitoring of each patient's health status to prevent unnecessary transfers to an acute care setting (Kocher et al 2011). Short term (ST) and LTC centers utilize mid-level practitioners on a daily basis to assist in physician coverage. Advanced Practice Nurses (APN) and Physician Assistant (PA) may satisfy a major need in preventing unnecessary transfers of patients to an acute care setting. This is demonstrated by a Nurse's astute assessment and the subsequent evaluation by the midlevel practitioner which can intercept a transfer to a hospital for a dehydrated patient who has abnormal labs and exhibiting symptoms of dehydration. The practitioner can input orders that are carried out in the center instead of transferring a patient to a hospital. When a change in status is caught early, a simple order for placement of a peripheral IV, can allow an efficient swift rehydration to the patient. This type of intervention avoids subjecting a patient to an unnecessary transfer to an acute care setting for the same treatment. It is more comfortable for the patient to receive treatment in the center than to allow a lengthy wait in the emergency room. This also illustrates an excellent way of managing resources and the appropriating of Medicare and Medicaid dollars with a positive patient experience.

Today, LTC centers are carefully evaluated for their rate of patient re-hospitalization. This performance indicator is made public for viewing by the Centers for Medicare Services (CMS) website. Salida et al (2018) notes the new areas being followed by CMS in LTC facilities includes: "Re-hospitalization, emergency department visits and successful return to the Community."

The medical provider at the center is responsible for patient visits every 30 – 60 days. The DON and designated nursing staff monitor these medical visits to ensure the visits transpire on a regular basis, and that none of the patient visits are omitted. The physician documents each visit addressing all health status and signing the monthly physician orders. Employing mid-level practitioners in the post-acute setting is an effective method for the management of non-acute symptoms before they become an emergent transfer. Symptoms caught early prevent these problems from occurring. It is now the norm to see an Advanced Practice Nurse (APN) or a Physician Assistant (PA) accessible in a facility on a daily basis.

Resources

Kocher, P & Adashi, E.Y (2011). Hospital
Readmissions and the Affordable Care Act.
Paying for Coordinated Quality Care. Retrieved
from:
https://jamanetnetwork.com/journal/jama/art
icle-abstract/1104541.
doi:10.1001/jama.2011.1561

Patrick, S. W. & Freed, G. L. (2012). Intergenerational
Enrollment and Expenditure changes in
Medicaid: trends from 1991 to 2005. *BMC
Health Services Research*, *12*, 327. Retrieved
from: http://doi.org/10.1186/1472-6963-12-
327

Salida, D., Welmer, D.L., Shi., & Mukand, D.B., (2018)
Examination of the New Short-Stay Nursing
Home Quality Measures: Re-hospitalization,
Emergency Department Visit, and Successful
Returns to the Community. Retrieved from:
https://www.ncbi.nlm.nih.gov/pubmed/30015
53

CHAPTER FOUR

Nursing Functions

Learning Objectives

In this section the individual will gain knowledge on the different nursing roles in a LTC Center. Gaining an understanding of the various roles can foster a strong motivation to pursue growth opportunities, such as new positions or jobs, and to collaborate with others in novel ways.

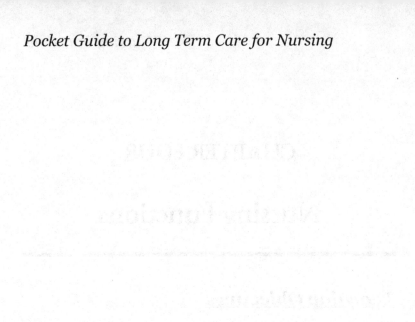

Nursing Supervisor

The role of the Nursing Supervisor is quite significant in the flow of LTC center functions, this individual performs as a mediator between the staff and upper management. The Nursing Supervisor reports to the DON and is in charge for the duration of the shift they work for example 7-3, 3-11 or 11-7 and could be termed as a mini-DON. A mini-DON acts as another eye and focus on all areas of significance. There are a variety of areas to manage like staffing to prevent patient care disruption and to assure a smooth operation ensues through the shift. Admissions to the center, communication with providers, reporting to the DON and administrator and patient safety for prevention of abuse. The DON may assign special projects for each Nursing Supervisor especially for areas being carefully monitored. The Nursing Supervisor addresses complaints promptly and reports any concerns of abuse to the respective parties immediately and follows with an investigation in a timely manner. They may also assist with staff education and any employee development or disciplinary issues. Most importantly the Nursing Supervisor sees to it that the patient care is carried out by rounding on all units. This task is also delegated to qualified staff members in the center. Rounding involves physically taking a walk on each unit and observe the activities and safety of each patient and assuring safety on the units.

Charge Nurse

The Charge Nurse has the responsibility of managing the care of their assigned patients, as well as, supervising CNA's on their units. The Charge Nurse makes sure all physician's orders are carried out in a timely manner. These orders may include, medication administration, treatments, and assessments, as well as, communicating any changes in the patient's condition with their medical provider. The Charge Nurse frequently dialogues with the Interdisciplinary Team members such as: dietary, physical therapy, occupational and speech therapy for the total care of each patient. The nurse ensures each patient attend all follow up appointments as directed by the discharge summary received from the hospital and/or any requests from any consult with a specialist outside the center. Additionally, the Charge Nurse ensures, other health care services are available to all the patients. These services may include dental, podiatry, audiology, ophthalmology and psychiatric needs.

The Charge Nurse also monitors mealtimes for safety and any diet appropriateness, along with, ensuring patient dignity is maintained. This involves providing meal time assistance at the appropriate eye level needed, providing options for clothing protectors and promoting a pleasant dining experience with ambient music appropriate for their age and generation. The Charge Nurse also carefully observes the proper care provided by the CNAs, observing the right technique with transfers, feeding, ambulation or incontinent care. Consistent communication concerning changes in patient condition and care are provided to the nursing supervisor, medical staff, and family members, for example reporting a pressure ulcer observation done by the Charge Nurse. The pressure ulcer prevention regimen put in place by the

DON is executed with the appropriate treatment recommendations by the Wound Care Nurse (WCN) and ordered by the MD for the type of wound. Following the DON's implemented system for prevention of pressure ulcer injuries helps to avoid new developments and reoccurrences of wounds that were healed. The Charge Nurse also diligently monitors patients at risk for falls, and safety in general.

On the day of admission, the Charge Nurse on duty completes the admission assessments with initial care plans, physician's orders, and treatments, along with orders for appropriate equipment necessary to allow the patient to function at their highest level possible. An initial fall risk assessment is completed an determines the level of care necessary to prevent a fall and subsequent injury. The CNA daily care cards are updated to reflect the required level of assistance needed for each patient. The Charge Nurse is responsible for overall patient care and coordinates other specialties such as Recreation, Pastoral care, and Psychiatric consultation alongside Dietary, Speech Therapy, Physical and Occupational Rehabilitation. A team approach is necessary to run more efficiently since most patient care tasks can be delegated to the appropriate team members. Sherman, Schwarzkopf, and Kiger (2011) confirm in their study that Charge Nurses have the responsibility of managing the staff, and additionally assuring patient care needs are fulfilled.

Staff Development Coordinator

The Role of the Staff Development Coordinator (SDC) serves as an educator for all staff in the center, providing training and education needs. The SDC nurse coordinates orientation to the center for newly hired staff members, and performs annual mandatory staff education and training, including the introduction of new topics, and nursing procedures, including, determining the nursing staff competencies for all nursing procedures performed in the center. The SDC is also tasked with the education and any miscellaneous staff training required for the plan of correction from the annual survey. Depending on the center census, a LTC center may combine the SDC and

IPN nursing roles, while other centers may also include wound care to the responsibilities. An SDC and IPN functioning in all these roles collectively require excellent organizational skills to evaluate and implement all staff training in addition to the monitoring of infections and wound care. Initial training and follow up education are completed annually and are recorded for compliance for all the nursing staff. Orientation introduces new employees to the corporate and LTC center policies and procedures. New Orientation Education includes Health Insurance Portability and Accountability Act, (HIPAA) requirements, Corporate Compliance, Occupational Safety and Health Administration (OSHA) requirements for State and Federal Government Standards for compliance expectation and understanding of all the federal and state standards of operation. Educational training includes abuse and neglect. CMS requires that a LTC center develop educational materials and training in prevention of abuse. (CMS, nd). Other types education includes: Emergency plans, Dignity and Privacy, Resident Rights, Fire Safety, Hazardous workplace protocols, Workplace Violence, Blood Borne Pathogens, Infection Control, Personal Protective Equipment (PPE), Handwashing, Occupational Exposure to Tuberculosis (TB), Pain Management, Dementia Training, Mouth Care, Sexual Harassment, and any additional center training needed. The SDC also ensures that new employees succeed through their probationary period by obtaining constructive feedback from others in charge with random monitoring of performance throughout the probationary period.

The SDC corrects any performance concerns that may arise through educating the employee; this effort helps to ensure a successful transition for the new staff member. All licensed staff must possess an up-to-date certification for Basic Life Support (BLS), IV Administration Certification and any other certification or competency required for the center specialty, for example, Peritoneal Dialysis, Negative Pressure Would Vacuum (NPWV), Left Ventricular Assistive Device (LVAD) and any special respiratory procedures. Frequent audits are performed on required staff certifications. The SDC may coordinate with outside contractors to provide the training required for the specific certification needed. Along with assuring these competencies are met, The SDC must document the training provided in each area for each nursing staff employee and have it available for surveyors. The educational recording system should be easily retrievable by utilizing a spreadsheet in an excel document, or a binder, or a software that is specifically designed for record keeping and maintained and updated ongoing as necessary. All training is logged by course title completion date and total time. The SDC prepares a monthly calendar for display in the center to inform all staff members of any upcoming training. Some educational topics may be developed by the SDC, but lack of time and other responsibilities may hinder a prompt execution; outsourcing may be the most suitable option. This can be provided by a health care product company or the contracted pharmacy abiding by compliance guidelines. There are outside entities that provide training and certification therefore, staff members are allowed time off to accomplish these training requirements. Education by the SDC may be formal or informal, a formal setting may include training at a general orientation and informally done on the nursing unit. Continuing education and training are very important in LTC setting and the SDC is pivotal in making sure the education needs of all staff members are met annually and periodically.

Certified Nursing Assistants

Certified Nursing Assistants (CNAs) are entrusted to provide direct care to patients and are often the first to discover and report any change in a patient's condition. They assist with bathing, toileting, oral hygiene, dressing, feeding, transfers, bed mobility, ambulation, and incontinent care. A CNA must be certified by the state and must possess a background free of criminal activity to secure employment in a LTC center. The center designated person manages this process while the SDC assures the annual state required education is maintained.

The staff training is recorded and reported to the state registry for compliance. The CNAs are supervised by the Charge Nurse on the daily routine of the unit providing guidance on any special situations, such as the days appointments outside the facility for any resident, vital signs, or any patient care needs. The CNA Care Card gives direction for all nursing care for each resident. CNAs must be informed of all patient care needs to ensure a seamless workflow on all shifts. CNAs must be updated on the following as they occur: important practice changes, modifications in the company or center processes, procedural updates, any new equipment, and any change in a patient's health condition. Clear direction and guidance in running a unit can contribute to employee retention, inclusive of, patient satisfaction and well-being. Parmelee, Laszlo, & Taylor (2009), mentioned that the cost of CNA turnover in the LTC setting can be around as high as $3,000 for each rehire and training. Therefore, the exemplary goal is to encourage employee retention. The CNA role is vital; the CNA needs to work closely under the direction of the Charge Nurse, to foster a smooth work flow and ensure professionalism and promote a good work environment. Below is an example of the information needed for the CNA to care for each patient on a Care Card Sample shown below in *fig 1.1*

CNA Care Card

Rm #	Name	Transfer Status/ Bed Mobility, Ambulation	Shower, Dressing , Toileting , Assist	Diet, Meal Assistance or set up	Fall Risk	Special needs	Other
512	Hold, Mark	Assist of one stand pivot transfer (SPT), and ambulation with rolling walker (RW)	Assist of one	Regular diet, thin liquids, set up, Fluid Restriction 1500ml	High fall risk	Patient is for early breakfast Mon, Wed and Fri - Dialysis Days	Call bell in reach, report any pain, frequent rounding

Fig 1.1

Documentation occurs each shift on each patient with utilization of an electronic record.

Minimum Data Set

The Minimum Data Set (MDS) is an assessment tool used to screen patients after entry into the center and used through to discharge. The tool is used to perform assessments on all patients admitted to a

45

LTC/STR center, regardless of the patient's insurance payor source or payor responsibility. The assessment is not based on a patient's source of payment or insurance coverage, but rather is a state and federal requirement to be utilized. An initial assessment is completed for each patient upon admission, then thereafter quarterly, annually and whenever there is a change in patient condition. These assessments are also done when a patient is transferred to an acute care setting, and upon return from the hospital. Interview assessments are conducted in person with all patients despite any inability to communicate from a disease process or a language barrier. Adaptive communication techniques may be used in event of a language barrier such as a language interpreter service. Resident care plan meetings are required for all patients where the status of the care plan is evaluated and adjusted to reflect the level of activity and nursing care needed. The care plan meeting must involve family members in the process where the interview assessment is discussed (CMS, 2012). The position of MDS Coordinator or Clinical Reimbursement Coordinator (MDSC/CRC) is a skilled position and one must be certified and experienced in this role. The function of this position requires skills of attention to detail to assure that all Medicare clients are certified to be in the center and maintain accuracy in the MDS assessments. The MDS Coordinator assures the MDS matches the documentation in the patient chart provided by nursing and the physicians. In areas where there are compliance concerns, the MDS Coordinator communicates with the nursing staff and makes sure correction and compliance changes are made. The nursing staff must chart accurately and timely, if errors are not identified, rejections may result in delay of reimbursement payments to the center. In addition, to the above duties, their role also requires them to assure care plans are in place for each new admission. A center may also require the MDS Coordinator to fill in as a nurse staff member or complete other staffing needs. Other centers may have too large a census to remove an MDS Coordinator periodically from their primary role. Although centers may require additional responsibility, it is very important that the MDSC/CRC person concentrates on their role.

Baseline Care Plans

Care plans direct the care needs of each patient. An individualized care plan, specific to the patient's individual care needs are mandatory. The care plan in a synopsis details the medical need for admission to the facility. The care plan is comprised of several things: a problem, a goal and at least three interventions to achieve each goal. Each care plan must also address the following: skin care, fall prevention interventions, activities of daily living (ADLs), any contact precautions, pain control, plan for discharge, anticoagulation therapy, any fluid overload concerns related to Congestive Heart Failure (CHF), nutrition concerns, dialysis patients and any specific admitting diagnoses. Care plans are updated at intervals when there is any change in condition. This must include any new problems identified with the appropriate intervention put in place. When a problem is resolved, the care plan is edited to reflect the new change. Care plans allows all parties caring for the patient to be informed of any new interventions and updates. The care plan mirrors, in some part the CNA care card with new interventions and update in status and care needs. Effective November 2017, the Center for Medicare Services (CMS) requires that baseline care plans be completed within 48 hours of admission to the center. These care plans are extracted from physician orders on admission which include dietary needs, diagnosis, therapy, and any data gathered from patients and their families. The individual care plan should address current medications, plan of care for the patient, goals for the patient, and any services to be provided by the facility. After a comprehensive care plan is completed, communication regarding status and changes must be made available to the patient and their family within 48 hours (AANAC, 2018).

Each center has an MDS Coordinator that completes and transmits the assessment after completion from all departments. The various sections of the MDS are alphabetically labeled and completed by multiple departments, such as the following areas: Social Service, rehabilitation department, dietary and nursing. The assessment is then checked for accuracy by the MDS Coordinator. Once completed and approved, it is then submitted to the Center for Medicare Services (CMS). The DON is kept informed of the status of the monthly submissions and monitors the quality of the assessments. The use of the electronic medical records allows for a smooth, and seamless documentation of nursing and medical data.

Resources

AANAC, (2018) Baseline Care plans and the 48 Hour
Rule: CMS Gives AANAC Some Insights.
Retrieved from:
https://www.aanac.org/Information/LTC-
Leader-Newsletter/post/baseline-care-plans-
and-the-48-hour-rule-cms-gives-aanac-some-
insights/2018-01-31

CMS, (2012), Minimum

Data   Set,   Retrieved   from:
https://www.cms.gov/Research-Statistics-
Data-and-Systems/Computer-Data-and-
Systems/Minimum-Data-Set-3-0-Public-
Reports/index.html

CMS, (2017) State Operations Manual, Retrieved from:
https://www.cms.gov/Regulations-and-
Guidance/Guidance/Manuals/Downloads/som
107c05.pdf

CMS, (nd) https://www.cms.gov/Regulations-and-
Guidance/Guidance/Manuals/Downloads/som
107ap_pp_guidelines_ltcf.pdf

Parmelee, P. A., Laszlo, M. C., & Taylor, J. A. (2009). Perceived Barriers to Effective Job Performance Among Nursing Assistants in Long-Term Care. *Journal of the American Medical Directors Association*, *10*(8), 559–567. http://doi.org/10.1016/j.jamda.2009.05.001

Sherman, R. O., Schwarzkopf, R., & Kiger, A. J. (2011). Charge Nurse Perspectives on Frontline Leadership in Acute Care Environments. *ISRN Nursing*, *2011*, 164052. http://doi.org/10.5402/2011/164052

CHAPTER FIVE

Other Essential Nursing Functions

Learning Objectives

In this section the individual will learn of the different functions in the center, the important functions that allow the smooth flow of nursing processes such as: 1) Assessments on Admission, 2) Code status, 3) Medication and Treatment Administration, 4) The Electronic Medical Record, 5) Chart Audits, 6) Nursing Documentation and 7) Oral Hygiene.

Assessments on Admission

Initial admission assessments are required for every patient arriving to the LTC center. A complete nursing assessment from the cranium to phalanges is completed on any new or returning patient in a LTC center. The nurse completing the assessment must identify any abnormality within a minimum of two hours of arriving to the center. They must observe any injuries, skin tear, bruises, scars, and wounds prior to admission to the center and document any patient equipment or personal belongings no matter how small. The admitting nurse obtains medical history from the patient, and if possible, from any family member. The admission assessment includes vital signs (VS), all body systems, cognition, musculoskeletal, integumentary, gastrointestinal, neurological, genitourinary, cardiac, respiratory, and circulatory. Each system is carefully assessed, any system problem is identified and documented immediately. The admitting nurse must also obtain admission weights, careful auscultation of the heart, lungs and abdomen, palpation, and inspection of skin.

Admission documentation must also include peripheral pulses symmetry of body from head to toe, any hearing or vision impairment, their ability to transfer, ambulate, bed mobility, including ability to perform ADLs such as bathing, toileting, dressing, feeding themselves and any other activities. Subsequently the nurse communicates to the physician any nursing concerns and obtain any recommendations as appropriate. Patients admitted with wound care needs or surgical wounds are prioritized and the applicable treatment order is initiated on admission to ensure patient healing. The DON overseas this area and assures appropriate treatment, standards and policies are followed, which guides the process of care for each patient. It is imperative that the assessment is completed on the day of admission with accuracy for compliance purposes. Potential problems may develop that could impact the patient's rehabilitation if these assessment concerns are not immediately identified and addressed.

Initiation of initial orders is an area closely observed during the annual survey process. For instance, if a patient has a cognitive deficit, and a history of dementia, appropriate care is needed to improve or maintain their cognitive and physical status. Any decline in the patient's health or cognition must be documented with appropriate interventions implemented and results monitored. Another example on admission concerns is failure to accurately assess a patient's skin and pinpoint any deviations from what's normal. If an area is not identified on the initial assessment, the patient can quickly develop a pressure ulcer or skin alteration that could have been prevented. Care plans should reflect interventions, in addition to, frequent monitoring for daily changes. There must be documentation of the following: recommendations, any new orders, treatments, medication changes, and outcomes in the patient's chart. An admission assessment is the outline in guiding future appropriate nursing care. All activities of daily living (ADL's) and functional assessments are also repeated prior to the patient discharge. CMS passed the "Improving Medicare Post-Acute Care Act of 2014" which emphasizes improvement in skin conditions, fall prevention and the functional, mental, and physical status in the LTC setting (CMS, 2016). Vaccination history is also maintained for each resident for the influenza, and pneumonia vaccines with the patient's signed consent and date of administration or declination recorded in the patient's medical record. Assessment of patient's psychiatric history is also completed and is done through the Pre-admission Screening and Resident Review (PASARR). Any recommendations from the PASARR screen is followed through with care and initiated on the day of admission (State Operations Manual, 2016). Improvement of the patient status report originates on admission. In order to have better patient outcomes the nursing staff must identify the care concerns, risks, and potential for decline and provide health care interventions to maintain consistency and achieve improvement goals.

These patient care areas are audited by the nursing department systematically as they carefully review each chart. The DON and ADON's oversite in this area, involves consistent follow up, applying nursing system improvements and monitoring through which assist in preventing deficiencies, citations or fines during the survey.

Code Status

A code status ensures that proper care is provided, and a patient's wishes are executed as directed by the specifications in their Advance Directives. The code status of a patient is addressed on admission to prevent any legal or ethical dilemmas from occurring. This is very significant since a change in condition could occur at any juncture in the patient's stay. Before performing Cardiopulmonary Resuscitation (CPR), knowledge of the code status of that patient is imperative. A patient's code status may be easily identified by an orange wrist band, or any system the LTC center implements. This is generally noted on the chart, both electronically and on paper. This document gives direction should the patient become incapacitated and unable to make an informed decision. The form is also signed by the patient and or the responsible party such as a family member and witnessed and completed with the physician's signature. If a patient's code status is not identified in a timely manner and in the event of a change in condition and need for CPR, it is then understood by all staff that the patient is a full code. A full code determines that the patient will have everything done to prolong their life. The patient Self Determination Act notes that facilities receiving reimbursement from Medicare or Medicaid must inform the patients of their right to choose lifesaving measures and provide education on planning for future care if incapacitation takes place (Castle, 1998). This is very important for all patients but especially those with co-morbidities and poor prognosis. Care plan meetings should always include the patients and family members and address the code status even if it remains the same. Discussion with the physician, family member and patient, should transpire for the best decisions to be made regarding the patient's wishes for the Advance Directive.

Medications and Treatments

Medication administration and treatments occurs on all shifts, from at least once per day, or multiple times per day, as ordered by the physician. The nursing staff is responsible and observes all medication and treatment standards. Medication and treatment carts are used to perform these tasks. Some LTC centers continue to use paper methods described as Kardexes for recording medication administration and treatments. Other centers may use a sophisticated Pyxis system to manage commonly used medications that are needed especially for new admissions until personal supplies arrive from the pharmacy. Medication and treatment carts are assigned to each wing of a center with patient medication supplies organized in each cart. During the LTC annual survey, the surveyor will request the medication administration times and personally observe each nurse during a medication pass to ensure the following. The surveyors observe the correct administration time, the right doses, the right patient, the right medication, the correct route, the right time, the right reason, the right response and the required documentation carried out by the nurse. The surveyor also takes note of infection control practices, patient privacy, and dignity during the med pass, including, proper disposal of unused medications and sharps used with a patient. The surveyor meticulously observes for medications that should not be crushed, medications that should be given with or without food or medications given separately. The surveyor watches whether a nurse introduces themselves, identify the patient with more than one identifier, and explain what is being administered. If using an Electronic Medical Record (EMR,) an updated patient photograph should be available and a legible wrist band with name and room number. At these observances, the surveyor will also determine the medication error rate for the center. This error rate should be less than 5%, if greater than that, the LTC center needs to. Initiate a corrective action and subsequent monitoring to be submitted as part of the report to the state to show compliance, improvement and patient protection from harm. The medication cart is to be kept clean, neat and organized with each patient medication. Each blister pack or medication pouch is labeled with the full name, dose, frequency schedule or time, medication name, expiration date, and route. Inhalers, nasal sprays or multi-dose medications are labeled with a patient identifier and placed in the patient's personalized pouch (Elizaiti, 2018) Under no circumstances should medication be borrowed or shared between patients. Patients, if deemed competent, may choose to administer their own medications under proper nursing supervision and should be assessed for competency and documented in the chart. Each nursing unit must have a medication room that stores and locks medications and med carts when not in use, including overstock medications. The medication storage room ideally should have a refrigerator to store refrigerated medications, with a double lock for narcotics plus a temperature log for monitoring and recording on a log sheet each shift to ensure the medication is kept at the appropriate temperature. IV supplies and biologicals are to be kept in the secured medication room and locked away from easy access.

A surveyor will inspect a medication room for cleanliness and organization, any deviation from standard will result in a citation. Treatment carts are similar to the medication cart but designed slightly different. LTC centers usually supply one or more carts for each unit depending on the number of patients. Treatment medications are also never shared, each patient's treatment is labeled and stored individually. Stocking the cart with supplies after performing the treatments is essential in preventing precious time wasted the next time treatments are done. A well-organized supply department coordinated with nursing on ordering supplies on time, lessens the problems for unavailable crucial treatment items to perform required nursing orders. Both medication and treatment carts need to be consistently well stocked by nursing with items required to perform medication administration and or treatments. Missing a medication or a treatment order can result in a preventable error.

The Electronic Medical Record

An Electronic Medical Record (EMR) replaces most paper records for documenting patient care. This means of documentation is utilized with medication administration, nurse's notes, physician's orders, and patient care plans. The Affordable Care Act (ACA) in

2010 required Healthcare settings to eliminate paper records (Adkinson and Chung 2014). The transition to an electronic method of medication administration is costly. Kruse, Mileski & Chidambaram (2017) discuss the difficulty of transitioning from paper to an EMR, including, the increasing cost of maintaining an EMR. There are still LTC centers that operate on a paper system, whereby the medications are administered from Kardexes (paper documentation). Prior to the Electronic Medication Administration Record (EMAR), all documentations and physician orders were completed on paper. Medical record Kardexes were created by a contracted pharmacy to provide paper-based Medication Administrative Records (MAR) and Treatment Administration

Records (TAR) upon request. The daunting task of preparing order entry records was laborious. Each month the paper Kardexes were delivered by the contracted Pharmacy. The staff would then edit and update the Kardexes with changes for new or, discontinued orders, or any order changes. The implementation of the EMR has greatly simplified the process of creating monthly records. Since the enactment of the mandatory EMR, orders are generated on a monthly basis by the center, as opposed to obtaining them from a pharmacy. The costs of creating these electronic documents have lessened drastically for center budgets. EMRs are quickly updated and are far more efficient in the delivery of medication administration. Although the ease of EMR is an improvement, there must be oversight and systems in place to monitor accuracy, patient privacy and still maintain patient safety to decrease medication errors.

Prevention of medication errors is ensured by checking the accuracy of data entered. Correct doses of medications, identification of patient allergies is essential to keeping patients safe. One method that has been unquestionable over the years has been the 24-hour check. This is completed on the 11-7 nursing shift and involves auditing and verifying physician orders from the previous shift to verify each order was correctly transcribed and carried out. 24-hour checks were previously done on paper and is still an effective practice of checking the EMR. A paper back-up system for EMR's is required and plans must be in place for potential outage, system software problems and computer malfunctions in the event this occurs.

Nursing Documentation

Nursing documentation involves chronicling a patient's condition throughout their stay in the center, with changes in condition, interventions, and responses to interventions. This documentation also includes: new and discontinued physician orders, test results, MD notifications and recommendations. The documentation provides proof that orders by the physician were indeed executed. Failure to document any of these areas may result in several negative outcomes. At any time, patient charts may be examined by insurance companies, or the state and federal government agencies who all reimburse for services. Lack of proper documentation and recording or any omissions could result in delay or forfeiture of payments. Lockwood (2017), mentions in her course the well-known adage: "if it was not documented, it was not done." The writer also mentions the importance of documenting changes in condition and the matching interventions, outcomes, or concerns brought up by the patients and their families. The patient record should indicate whether any concerns were resolved and the specific action taken to rectify the problem. Appropriate legally approved abbreviations must be utilized in all nursing documentation. Alshaikn, (2012) notes the percentage of medication errors reported in the United States (US) are related to unsafe abbreviations. With the EMR in place, there is less need to decipher hand writings as in the past when hand written physician's orders or nurse's notes caused confusion with abbreviations, resulting in serious errors or death. Tariq et al (2023) mention thousands of patients die from medication errors. The consistent use of an EMR form of documentation assist in displaying accurate and timely documentation. EMR developers have also integrated stoppers, checks and alerts to prevent these errors from occurring. The Electronic Health Record (EHR) can improve the quality of care in LTC facilities, reduce medication errors, and improve clinical documentation and decision making.

Chart Audits

Chart audits are critically important to monitoring adequate care of each patient. They are performed at each new admission and periodically on current patients, both electronically and in paper form. Electronic audits help to ensure that all chart requirements are in place. The chart audits query errors and help identify any missed patient interventions. Care plans should reflect appropriate orders, diagnoses, ability to function, cognitive deficits, any psychiatric problems, risk for skin break down, risk for fall, deficits in any ADL's, appropriate nursing notes, any allergies, and any medication reconciliation needed. Each patient's chart must reflect a code status that is signed by the patient's physician, the patient and/or responsible party. The code status of each patient is distinguished on admission to prevent any ethical dilemmas.

Another important area audited is pain management which is a major focus during the survey. The study conducted by Jablonski and Ersek (2009) used retrospective chart audits to identify whether pain management in a LTC center was evidence based. The practice standard findings revealed a distance between how pain is managed and current evidence-based practice; the retrospective study revealed very important gap issues. It is critical to perform chart audits timely so any potential problem in patient care or errors can be pinpointed and the necessary corrections made ahead of time. It is better to correct any errors early, rather than have a domino effect of challenges later. The process of chart audits also ensures physician visits are carried out shortly after admission, along with any change in condition documented at the time of the visit, and periodic visits required by state regulations. CMS, (2017) requires that the chart accurately reflect the current condition of the patient and show evidence with documentation of the patient's current status before and after any interventions. Any change in condition or recommendations for other treatment must be documented. Chart audits are time consuming, especially, if it is a busy LTC center with many admissions and discharges. However, when done systematically it will prevent any omissions, errors and allow any patient safety concerns to be addressed quickly. Patient records should also be accessible for review by state surveyors during health inspections; some records may be patients who have discharged from the center. These overflow records are maintained by the Medical Records Department.

Oral Hygiene

Oral health is of profound significance in the elderly population. Many of the patients in this population are totally dependent on a caregiver and require assistance with oral hygiene and many other ADL's. As patients age, some may lose permanent teeth and eventually use dentures. They may over time have ill-fitting dentures from shrinking gums. The care plan must detail three things: the type of assistance a patient needs, how much assistance is needed and how often it should be performed. McNally et al (2012) discussed the importance of oral hygiene in the LTC environment and notes that lack of mouth care can considerably contribute to certain sicknesses, such as, respiratory illnesses. The oral bacteria accumulate overnight and performing careful oral hygiene can eliminate microbes and avoid illness.

The writers also mention several types of excuses that arise commonly to not provide mouth care for the patient in need, such as, lack of staffing, not enough time or too many patients to provide care for. The U.S. Department of Health and Human Services (USDHS) has made oral health a major focus and note the impact on quality of life and the ability to eat (U.S Department of Health and Human Services Oral Health Coordinating Committee, 2016). The inability to eat affects nutrition, nutrition impacts weight while the aim is to prevent weight loss and illnesses. One of the ways to prevent these unfavorable outcomes is to provide good oral hygiene. In addition, training on good mouth care, careful monitoring, and regular dental services to assist in preventing these conditions is crucial. Providing good oral care allows the nursing staff to identify issues such as ill-fitting dentures, mouth pain and cavities. Identifying these important facts makes for quick intervention and preventative care to avoid further decline of oral health.

Resources

Adkinson, J. M., & Chung, K. C. (2014). The Patient Protection and Affordable Care Act: A Primer for Hand Surgeons. *Hand Clinics, 30*(3), 345–vii. http://doi.org/10.1016/j.hcl.2014.05.002

https://www.aanac.org/Information/Baseline-Care-Plan/post/baseline-care-plan-faqs-weekends-required-revisions-and-other-issues/2017-10-16

Alslaikh, M; Mayet A, Ahmed, Y, Aljadlhey, H, (2012) Intervention to Reduce the use of Unsafe Abbreviations in a Teaching Hospital. Saudi publication of the Saude Pharmaceutical Society. 21(3) 277-28. doi: 10.1016/j.jsps.2013.10.006

Castle, N. G., & Mor, V. (1998). Advance care planning in nursing homes: pre- and post-Patient Self-Determination Act. *Health Services Research, 33*(1), 101–124.

Elizaitis, B (2018) Ftag 761 Label/storage, Drug Biologicals. Retrieved from:

https://cmscompliancegroup.com/2018/03/0
9/ftag-of-the-week-f761-label-store/

CMS, (2016), Patient Assessment Instruments,
Retrieved from:
https://www.cms.gov/Medicare/Quality-
Initiatives-Patient-Assessment-
Instruments/NursingHomeQualityInits/Downl
oads/PBJ-Summary-Presentation.pdf

CMS, (2016), Post-Acute care initiatives, Retrieved
from: https://www.cms.gov/Medicare/Quality-
Initiatives-Patient-Assessment-
Instruments/Post-Acute-Care-Quality-
Initiatives/PAC-Quality-Initiatives.html

CMS, (2017) State Operations Manual, Long term Care
Facility, Retrieved from:
https://www.cms.gov/Regulations-and-
Guidance/Guidance/Manuals/downloads/som
107ap_pp_guidelines_ltcf.pdf

Jablonski, A., & Ersek, M. (2009). Nursing Home Staff
Adherence to Evidence-Based Pain
Management Practices. *Journal of*

Gerontological Nursing, 35(7), 28–37. http://doi.org/10.3928/00989134-20090701-02

Kruse C., S., Mileski M, Vijaykumar A., G., Viswanathan SV, Suskandla U, Chidambaram Y, (2017) Impact of Electronic Health Records on Long-Term Care Facilities: Systematic Review JMIR Med Inform;5(3):e35. DOI: 10.2196/medinform.7958

Lockwood, W. (2017). Documentation: Accurate & Legal; Retrieved from: http://2017rn.org.

McNally, M. E., Martin-Misener, R., Wyatt, C. C. L., McNeil, K. P., Crowell, S. J., Matthews, D. C., & Clovis, J. B. (2012). Action Planning for Daily Mouth Care in Long-Term Care: The Brushing Up on Mouth Care Project. *Nursing Research and Practice, 2012,* 368356. http://doi.org/10.1155/2012/368356

State Operations Manual, (2016). Retrieved from: http://www.hpm.umn.edu/nhregsplus/Resources%20and%20Publications/CMS_Survey_Re

sources/CMS/Appx_SOM_483.30%20-
%20Nursing%20Service

Talley, K. M., Wyman, J. F., Savik, K., Kane, R. L.,
Mueller, C., & Zhao, H. (2015). Restorative
Care's Effect on Activities of Daily Living
Dependency in Long-stay Nursing Home
Residents. The Gerontologist, 55 Suppl 1(Suppl
1), S88–S98.
https://doi.org/10.1093/geront/gnv011

Tariq RA, Vashisht R, Sinha A, Scherbak Y. (2023)
Medication Dispensing Errors and Prevention.
National Library of Medicine. Retrieved from:
https://pubmed.ncbi.nlm.nih.gov/30085607/

U.S. Department of Health and Human Services Oral
Health Coordinating Committee. (2016). U.S.
Department of Health and Human Services Oral
Health Strategic Framework, 2014–
2017. *Public Health Reports, 131*(2), 242–257.

CHAPTER SIX

Important Center Functions

Learning Objectives

In this section discussion will take place on behind-the-scenes operations that are critical for functioning. Areas that will be covered specifically are the following: 1) Nursing Budget Management, 2) Medical Records Maintenance, 3) Temperature Logs, 4) Narcotic Management, 5) Unnecessary Drug Management, 6) Disposal of Medications, 7) Crash Cart and 8) Rounding.

Nursing Budget Management

Each department in a LTC center has its own budget either run on a fiscal year or an annual year. LTC centers operate on a 24hour basis and adequate staffing must be scheduled for these hours. The nursing department's budget is the largest and includes the following: staffing, equipment purchases, items infrequently purchased such as medication carts, computers, vital sign machines, bladder scanner, or an EKG machine. Necessary items used on a daily basis, such as, dressing supplies, medication, over the counter purchases, IV medications, and some of the ancillary supplies such as, IV tubing and pumps, Normal Saline (NS) flushes, caps, alcohol wipes and IV labels. Staffing budgets involve both full time employees (FTE) and part time employees (PTE), with patient per day (PPD) care needs. Staffing vacancies, frequent turnovers, overtime and replacement of equipment, also add greatly to the nursing budget in a sizeable way. Nursing budgets are carefully monitored by the DON and kept within the center budgetary parameters, whether it's a for profit or non-profit LTC establishment. Wilson et al, (2014) discuss the changes in healthcare to provide the highest quality of care with the lowest cost possible. If the center is overseen by a corporate entity, there must be explanation or reasons for over budgeting in any specific area to the governing establishments. There are circumstances that can affect the budget periodically; specifically, the unpredictability of the census, admissions and discharges, and equipment failure. Part of the role of the DNS is to propose a nursing budget for the upcoming year which suggest dollar amounts for each area, such as the following: education, orientation, new hires, training, medical, office expenses, pharmacy expenses, patient care supplies and supplemental staffing projections. The budget will generally be compared to the previous year with changes noted. Large item purchases may be postponed or put off, while other necessary areas in the center are prioritized. An example may be a major improvement to the center, such as the remodeling of patient rooms or patient areas. These may take precedence over obtaining new office furniture. Such prioritization promotes a positive patient experience.

Medical Records Maintenance

The Medical Records Department is very important in the overall management of patient record documentation and the preservation of LTC operations. The staff personnel in this role are meticulous and pays close attention to detail. Some centers may combine this role with another position depending on the center patient capacity and center needs.

All closed records from discharged patients are retained and secured in the Medical Records department and are readily retrievable upon demand. If patients have been in the center a long period of time, there may be overflow records. Charts are thinned and the overflow records are carefully stored for easy retrieval. Request for patient records occur frequently by various entities; these include: Medicare and Medicaid, legal offices, other insurance companies, patients and family members and during the annual Health Inspection survey process. Records must be managed systematically, and available always for speedy retrieval. The Medical Records department also prepares charts for new admissions and performing special audits on open charts frequently for completion, accuracy, and compliance. This process assures the patient medical record is in order.

Food and Refrigeration Temperature Logs

All refrigerator temperatures are monitored every shift, 24/7, 365 days per year. Monitoring medications of various kinds such as: IVs, liquid or capsules, food items, specimens etc. A record of temperature logs shows whether food items and medications are stored at the at appropriate temperature. Food items, medications and specimen are all stored in separate refrigerators. Refrigerators are placed in a medication room, dining room, kitchen or in a patients' room. The correct temperature prevents any medication from becoming unusable and protects food from spoilage. Items are discarded at the appropriate date to prevent an accidental consumption by a patient who potentially could develop a food borne illnesses. When a surveyor visits a center, one of the many items that is examined immediately upon entry are the refrigerators and temperature logs. Surveyors observe for cleanliness and that food items are checked for labeling and expiration date. The food items in the refrigerator should be dated and a system in place by housekeeping or the dietary department to discard food upon the expiration date. One good routine is to have pre-made labels to record the date the item was placed in the refrigerator and the date to discard. Each refrigerator temperature log is initiated at the beginning of the month for all food, medicine and specimens for lab tests. They are tracked daily with the date, temperature and with an initial. Omission of a temperature confirms lack of monitoring and this could reflect negatively in the eyes of a surveyor. Meticulous management of temperature logs is essential in management of medications and food at the right temperature.

Narcotic Management

Narcotic management is a significant priority for the DON. The Drug Enforcement Agency's (DEAs) strict monitoring and frequent audits are imperative to preventing narcotic diversion among nurses. In 2016, the "Ensuring Patient Access and Effective Drug Enforcement Act of 2016" no longer allows for a registrant's license to be suspended prior to determining any serious threats to patient safety. This still requires a LTC center to have a system in place to prevent drug diversion. Drug diversion is harmful in many ways, not only to the staff, but also harmful to the patient. Schaefer & Perez, (2014) notes diversion of drugs in healthcare can result in inadequate pain management for patients. Berge et al, (2012) also describe events of drug diversion which resulted in inadequate pain management during procedures. Some facilities operate a sophisticated Pyxis system for frequently used medications, overstock, and narcotic medications. EMR narcotics are printed on individual narcotic control sheets produced by the pharmacy supplier. On each shift, the narcotic medication count is verified and any error is reported immediately to the DON. The shift supervisor verifies the narcotic count is accurate for their shift and it is signed and witnessed, confirming that the count is correct. After an error is reported to the DON/ADON, and there is difficulty resolving the narcotic count, the DEA is notified. The DEA is responsible for monitoring of all drug diversion in healthcare facilities; any diversion is reported immediately. The process to obtain a new supply of narcotics is done by the DON through completing a Schedule II form, listing all the medication names with the quantity and doses to be requested from the pharmacy. The form is then signed by the Medical Director and sealed. This Schedule II form is then delivered to the pharmacy, filled, and returned to the center ASAP. When the narcotic is processed and delivered to the center it is received and signed by an RN and verified by two nurses. This is then secured under a double lock system. This management of narcotic is crucial in preventing diversions and maintaining compliance with the DEA standards.

Unnecessary Drug Management

Drug regimen reviews are pivotal for identifying unnecessary medications. Reviews are done on admission and periodically for polypharmacy by the consultant pharmacist. The LTC center must document any drug allergies, as well as the correct diagnosis for each medication. A center secures the services of a consultant pharmacist to perform a drug regimen review regularly addressing the above-mentioned items, and in addition, substantiate the correct diagnoses for each medication. The pharmacist performs a gradual dose reduction for Psychotropic drugs. The pharmacist may make recommendation for labs to be performed and document necessity for the drug, address the need to continue or suggest a dose reduction, even if, the attempt is futile. O'Shea et al (2017) discusses the task of completing a comprehensive medication review in the LTC setting as required by CMS. Unnecessary drugs are one of great importance and should be carefully kept under surveillance for poly pharmacy. Dose reduction should be recommended by the pharmacy consultant in conjunction with the center Physician, Nurse Practitioner (NP), or Physician's Assistant (PA). The nursing staff then ensures these medication recommendations are carried out. Not every patient may need a dose reduction. However, documentation showing the outcomes of the attempted reduction demonstrates this was attempted. Surveyors look for compliance and follow through with pharmacy and physician recommendations during the annual survey.

Drug Disposal

Disposal of medication involves discarding expired and discontinued medication in the form of liquids, pills, ampules, capsules, caplets, injections, IV fluids, inhalers, or treatment creams. Medication destruction is a time-consuming and labor-intensive task that must be completed regularly. This is completed for both regular and controlled drugs, the best approach is to complete the medication destruction monthly. The DON and ADON organize the efforts for drug destruction in a center. Strict guidelines must be followed for medication destruction of pills, inhalers, liquids, capsules, injections, intravenous meds, etc. The LTC facility follows each state's requirement for medication destruction since each state may differ in that the type of medication that may require disposal in a specific way. To foster an almost effortless monthly drug destruction, it is helpful to provide collection bins for collecting the drugs to be disposed of. The center should provide enough bins to sort and separate by type. Frequent collection from each unit helps to prevent a gross overflow. The narcotics are logged on a spreadsheet with the prescription number, dose, prescribing physician, name of medication, and the dispensing pharmacy along with the total amount to be destroyed. The destruction is accomplished by using a heavy-duty pill shredder with the capability to destroy a whole blister pack and individual pills. Other medications may be disposed of according to the state regulations. Completion of the process is finalized by both signatures on the Narcotic log listing all medications that were discarded by name, dose and amounts. Medications are not discarded by pouring into a sewer system. Boleda, Alechaga, Moyano, et al. (2014) state that pharmaceutical products in the local water system can be problematic and hard to eliminate. Disposing of medications through the sewer system contaminates the drinking water since the medications often times cannot be removed from the water supply. Medication destruction is a great undertaking, as well as, a major expense. Chamberlain, (2019) discussed the consequences by the Environmental Protection Agency (EPA) for improper destruction of pharmaceutical products, whereby fines potentially can be in the thousands. It is advisable that a center contracts with a company for medication disposal and follow the state standards for destruction. It is a practice in some states that certain unused medications can be returned to the pharmacy for credit according to the Center for Medicare and Medicaid Services (2004), this practice helps in a small way with medication waste.

Crash Carts

Crash carts are supplied and stocked with emergency supplies in the event that a patient in medical distress becomes unconscious and a code is initiated. The crash cart is utilized during the code. It is infrequent that a crash cart is used on a daily basis in a Short-Term Rehabilitation (STR) or Long-Term Care (LTC) center; for this reason, meticulous monitoring is important to ensure needed supplies are current and available daily. Depending on the facility protocol, the crash cart itemized list is checked each shift assuring that all supplies are available and items on the cart have not expired. The sheet is then signed off by each nurse completing the check. Collaboration with the supply department should be ongoing to keep supplies available and current. Each licensed staff is responsible for keeping track of this important task. After the cart is used, items are replaced immediately for the next occurrence. Documentation of shift checks could be requested by a surveyor if a random check reveals missing nursing entries on the code cart; the facility may incur a citation or fine for the deficiency. Care must be taken to assure this is attended to on every shift.

Rounding

Rounding involves touring each nursing unit to assure nursing care is being provided in a timely manner and by appropriate nursing standard. This can be done by the Nursing Supervisor or anyone on the leadership team each shift. Rounding is an opportunity to observe any safety concerns, patient care needs, customer complaints, interviews in addressing concerns, monitor hallways for compliance with cleanliness and decluttering in the event of an emergency. Included in the rounds is also observation at mealtimes to assure proper assistance is provided to each resident and that each person is accommodated appropriately with the staff member assisting at eye level for each meal. Observance of staff and patient interaction helps to ascertain that patient dignity and privacy is always maintained. Patients should be respected and referred to their given name and not descriptions, such as, "Honey", or "Darling" which is demeaning. Meaningful respectful interaction should occur between the staff and patient daily. While rounding, concerns can be quickly identified and addressed timely. On rounding attention should also be focused on a patients' appearance, appropriate attire in their location, cleanliness of their hair, and whether shaved or not, as well as clean clothing. Based on any center challenges it may warrant that rounding be accomplished more frequently and at various times especially at the change of shift in order to view shift proceedings and assure patient care needs are attended to swiftly. This task can appropriately be delegated to other capable nursing staff members. Some LTC centers have implemented hourly rounding done by the nursing leadership as a measure to meet the immediate needs of patients and to maintain a safe environment at all times. Mitchell et al (2014) stressed how hourly rounding affects nursing care positively. The writer notes that rounding on patients more frequently helps to address basic needs like timely toileting which enhances the patient experience.

Resources

Berge, K. H., Dillon, K. R., Sikkink, K. M., Taylor, T. K., & Lanier, W. L. (2012). Diversion of Drugs Within Health Care Facilities, a Multiple-Victim Crime: Patterns of Diversion, Scope, Consequences, Detection, and Prevention. *Mayo Clinic Proceedings, 87*(7), 674–682. http://doi.org/10.1016/j.mayocp.2012.03.013

Boleda, M.R., Alechaga, É., Moyano, E. et al. (2014) Environ Sci Pollut Retrieved from: https://doi.org/10.1007/s11356-014-2885-9, 21: 10917.

Chamberlain, (2019). Consequences of Improperly Disposed Pharmaceuticals. Retrieved from: https://www.danielshealth.com/knowledge-center/pharmaceutical-improper-disposal-consequences.

Center for Medicare and Medicaid Services, (2004) CMS Review of Current Standards of Practice for Lon-Term Care Pharmacy Services. Long-

Term Care Pharmacy Primer, Retrieved from: https://www.cms.gov/Research-Statistics-Data-and-Systems/Statistics-Trends-and-Reports/Reports/Downloads/LewinGroup.pdf

Mitchell, M. D., Lavenberg, J. G., Trotta, R., & Umscheid, C. A. (2014). Hourly Rounding to Improve Nursing Responsiveness: A Systematic Review. *The Journal of Nursing Administration*, *44*(9), 462–472. Retrieved from: http://doi.org/10.1097/NNA.0000000000000101

O'Shea, T.E., Zarowitz, B. J., & Erwin, W. G., 2017. Comprehensive Medication Reviews in Long-term Care Facilities: History of Process Implementation and 2015 Results. *Journal of Managed Care & Specialty Pharmacy*, 23:1, 22-26

Schaefer, M. K., & Perz, J. F. (2014). Outbreaks of infections associated with drug diversion by US health care personnel. *Mayo Clinic proceedings, 89*(7), 878-87.

Talyst.com, (2009) Retrieved from http://www.talyst.com/wp content/uploads/Talyst_White_Paper_Medication_Waste_LTC.pdf

Wilson, M. G., Ellen, M. E., Lavis, J. N., Grimshaw, J. M., Moat, K. A., Shemer, J., … Samra, K. (2014). Processes, contexts, and rationale for disinvestment: a protocol for a critical interpretive synthesis. *Systematic Reviews, 3,* 143. http://doi.org/10.1186/2046-4053-3-143

CHAPTER SEVEN

Contracted Services

Learning Objectives

Contracted services are essential for the residents that are in the center. When residents are not able to go into the community the necessary services must be provided in the center. Those services are the following: 1) Pharmacy Services, 2) Podiatry, 3) Audiology, 4) Optometry, 5) Psychiatry, 6) Diagnostic Services, 7) Dental Services, 8) Wound Care, 9) Respiratory Services and 10) Other Services.

Contracted Services

Contracted services are provided by outside entities to meet the needs of the center. The center forms a contractual agreement specifying the agreed upon terms for the following services:

1) Dental/Dentist and Hygienist, 2) Psychiatry 3) Podiatry, 4) Audiology, 5) Optometry, 6) Pharmacy, 7) Diagnostic, 8) Wound Care 9) Respiratory and 10) Other Services.

A patient exhibiting minimal progress after receiving therapy for some time who has plateaued and has been in the center greater than a hundred days are deemed categorized as a LTC resident. Services that would customarily be provided in the community must be made available to the residents. The resident may opt to take advantage of community services but cannot be denied services within the center. If the patient prefers services in the community, the necessary arrangements are made to accommodate this request and provide any transportation needed to and from those services. Careful and diligent record keeping is done to prevent patients from being overlooked for any timely services that were recommended. Some contractors as a courtesy may track patient services from a census list provided by the center to the vendor who provides these needed services. The vendor in turn sends out reminders to the center when services are due for a particular patient. However, these reminders may be unreliable, due to frequent census changes in admissions and discharges. The need for services may be identified by a family member, nursing staff, or the patient themselves. Payer source is important, since reimbursement will be based on specific plan benefits for private insurance, Medicaid, and Medicare. Inquiry must be made to determine the coverage by each plan. In each case, consent must be obtained from either a family member or the patient with a physician's order in the chart. Other contracted services may include a Wound Consultant, Respiratory services, or any other specialty services specific to a center. CMS, (2017) requires that routine services, as well as emergent services be provided for each patient. A patient's service records may be examined in detail, specifically, services provided or unmet. The DON designates a licensed nurse to oversee the continued services are provided as needed. Charge nurses are also responsible for keeping this area in check. Contracted services are reviewed thoroughly by surveyors and can become a focus of concern during the survey process if omissions are noted in the documentation and record keeping.

Optometry Services

Optometry care is another necessary service that is provided for each resident in the LTC facility. This service is scrutinized for the frequency of visits and service to the residents. During the annual survey the charts are reviewed for compliance. Providing eye care adds to the quality of life and assists in preventing falls or accidents. Geriatr, (2011) mentions the importance of providing eye care. Quick identification of eye problems can follow early intervention and improved quality of care allowing the resident to perform at their highest level of function.

Dental and Hygiene Services

On admission a patient is assessed to determine their dental status and is immediately placed on the rotation to be seen by the dentist and hygienist. Residents are assessed for caries, any missing teeth, use of dentures and if they fit appropriately. In addition, note any mouth injury or any complaints of pain. An assigned licensed nurse will coordinate the dental visits and assure that patients needing the services are provided in a timely manner. Chart audits are done to assure the services are being provided on schedule. The chart must have an MD order and the record must show that services requested were signed by the resident or the family member along with the payer source on record. After a visit by the provider the needed services rendered will be documented to report the condition of the patient's mouth and any recommendations. The nursing staff is responsible for carrying out the physician's orders. Providing dental and hygiene services are vital to the health of each resident since these services prevent diseases in patients. Vishnevsky, (2013) notes the health benefit in preventing heart disease from periodontal bacteria. Importantly, oral hygiene should be provided on a daily basis especially after each meal. For those with dentures the center must develop a system that prevents dentures from being lost. Dentures can potentially get lost in the laundry, trash, or the dinner tray. Elizaitis, (2018) notes if dentures become lost the LTC center has 72 hours to schedule an appointment with a dentist and devise a plan of care for the resident to eat. If not done in a timely fashion documentation must reveal reasons for the postponement.

Podiatry Services

Similar to other contracted services, a patient is assessed to determine the condition of their feet, any wounds, scars, ill-fitting shoes or any hindrances to ambulation and independence. The goal of care is to assist the resident to reach their highest level of function. The podiatrist will perform services, such as, toenail trimming, especially for diabetics. They will assess for custom made shoes plus address corns and calluses. Contracted services are carefully monitored by the surveyors and documentation must be evident that the service is provided on a regular basis and as needed. Hinkes, (2009) discusses the importance of the role a Podiatrist in the quick identification of problems before they get worse or develop the need for more serious interventions like an amputation.

Audiology Services

Part of the initial assessment on admission is to determine the hearing capabilities of a patient and assess if they are hard of hearing and dependent on using hearing aids. A patient may be admitted with normal hearing and may develop a hearing loss over time. Hearing loss may develop through medications administered and regular assessment for hearing is important. Center for Medicare Advocacy, (2020) note that failure to address hearing early may pose a risk for increased Dementia, increased fall risk and prone to depression. There are some medications that cause a loss of hearing such as aspirin, NSAIDS namely Ibuprofen, antibiotics, chemotherapy drugs such as Cisplatin, carboplatin, and bleomycin; loop diuretics such as Lasix and Bumetanide (Gilchrist, 2015). Even more important is that the hearing checks are performed on schedule. Surveyors eye closely services provided for hearing aids which are to be provided by the Audiologist for compliance.

Pharmacy Services

Pharmacy services are provided offsite; a LTC Center does not have an onsite pharmacy to provide medications for the patients admitted. Instead, most LTC centers contract with an outside pharmacy. Medications are ordered by transmitting the physician's orders to the pharmacy, and once the pharmacy has delivered the supplies, they are then distributed to the units. Consultation with the pharmacist is also available as part of the services offered to the facility to evaluate a patient's medication regimen to prevent polypharmacy. The pharmacist makes recommendations for eliminating unnecessary medications and assuring the correct diagnoses matches each patient's medication order. If a center utilizes Kardexes, they are normally supplied for each admission throughout the month. Pharmacy deliveries occur at agreed upon times by the center and the pharmacy. Each patient medication comes individually labeled and packaged with the patient's name, physicians name and prescribing expiration date, the prescription number, the medication name, dose, and administration schedule. Centers utilizing an EMR are only supplied medications when ordered, no paper Kardex's are necessary. Over the counter (OTC) that are not available from the pharmacy may be ordered from a different supplier.

Pharmacy policies must specify directions for how pharmacy services are coordinated with the center. This specifically applies to medication administration, how documentation is completed, policies on medication destruction, how controlled drugs are received, distribution and recording of all the patient medication (CMS, 2017). The pharmacy may also write center specific policies for STR or LTC facilities. Even though pharmacy services are provided by the center, patients may choose their own pharmacy, if they prefer. The DON makes sure systems are in place to monitor pharmacy services in compliance with the State and Federal requirements. In these ways the pharmacy plays a major role for patients admitted to the center by providing consultation and important lifesaving medications.

Psychiatric Services

Psychiatric services are necessary to address patients with Depression, Anxiety, Borderline Personality Disorder, Dementia, Schizophrenia, or any other behavioral problems. A STR may focus on admitting patients with multiple medical co-morbidities and post-surgical patients. However, they may have underlying psychological complications, and may exhibit uncontrollable behaviors, others may exhibit depression or anxiety. These symptoms may not have been previously addressed or may have been poorly managed prior to admission. Whatever the history, when patients are admitted to any facility, psychiatric concerns or diagnosis must be addressed. Psychiatric management is offered to both LTC and STR settings. A patient may request the service or may be referred by a nursing staff because of behaviors manifested. Merely consulting with a psychiatrist or NP, adjusting a medication dose, introducing a different medication or introducing non-medication interventions can be helpful for a patient with a Psychiatric problem. Simple interventions may make a great difference. Martin, Ham and Hilton, (2018) note that nurses frequently use non-pharmaceutical interventions for a patient's psychiatric problems, such as, a teaching opportunity or diminishing a situation to prevent it from worsening. Each patient should be assessed, determine triggers to the unwanted behaviors and provide treatment. With that information, an individual care plan is constructed along with the appropriate interventions to be carried out. Thomas et al (2014) discusses the significance of the management of psychiatric treatment and careful assessment of the hidden problems prior to administering any psychiatric drug. Clear documentation from both nurses and physicians should reveal the history and effects of interventions reflecting positive or negative changes, and if, favorable outcomes were met.

This area is closely monitored by the DON/ADON throughout the year and is examined during the survey process. The definitive purpose in medication management of psychological patients is to reduce the use of psychotropic medications and initiate the most effective intervention. Percentages of psychotropic drug usage are reflected in the 5-star rating and are available for public view at cms.gov. The fewer number of patients on psychotropic medications, the more favorable the ratings are for the center. Great nursing care involves observing and aiming to heal the whole person. Psychiatric services are provided and are necessary for the reduction of these medications. Scrutiny each month helps to reduce medication use to more acceptable levels.

Diagnostic Services

Traditionally, orders are written for tests to be performed which are generally not available on site but must be made available for the residents. These may involve labs due daily, weekly, or monthly and PRN; X-rays ordered STAT or a Doppler Ultrasound. These orders must be delivered timely, contact must be made to the company that provides these services for timely completion; it is highly unacceptable to delay communication for the necessary services to be provided and executed.

Wound Care Services

Wound Care services may be provided by an outside provider or within the center. A center may manage their wounds in house by a Wound Care Nurse (WCN) and a provider, as well as one who does wound rounds with the nursing staff. Unmanageable wounds can be treated in the community by a wound specialist who provides advanced treatments such as debridement or Hyperbaric oxygen therapy for wounds. Wound care is significant, the rate of wounds in a center reflects the care that is being provided. Systems must be in place for wound prevention and for interventions when a wound develops to achieve the goal of keeping the center wound rate at a minimum.

Respiratory Services

Respiratory services can range from providing oxygen to those needing ongoing therapy all the way to ventilated patients with Tracheostomy's or routine nebulizer breathing treatments. Patients requiring ongoing care and monitoring, assuring all equipment runs smoothly and troubleshoot when necessary. Not all centers provide care for Ventilated patients. Centers that provide this service, must hire a Respiratory Therapist. They do not have to be scheduled 24 hours per day but when not on scheduled, the nurses carry out the treatment modalities.

Other Services

Other services provided are laundry and hair care. Families may opt to do their loved one's laundry, if they choose. Hair care is provided on a weekly basis by securing a hairdresser or a barber from the community. A designated room must be made available by the center for services to be conducted by the hair stylist. These services are done by appointments or on a first com first serve basis.

<u>*Resources*</u>

Geriatr, (2011), An Optometrist- Led Eye Care
    Program for Older Residents of Retirement
    Homes & Long-Term Care Facilities. Retrieved
    from:
    https://www.ncbi.nlm.nih.gov/search/all/?ter
    m=An+Optometrist-
    +Led+Eye+Care+Program+for+Older+Reside
    nts+of+Retirement+Homes+%26+Long-
    Term+Care+Facilities.+

CMS, (2017) New Long-Term Care Survey, Retrieved
    from https://www.cms.gov/site-search/search-
    results.html?q=new%20long%20term%20care
    %20survey

Elizaitis, B., (2018), Dental services in SNFs/NFs.
    Retrieved
    from:https://cmscompliancegroup.com/2018/
    06/29/ftags-of-the-week-f790-f791-dental/

Gilchist, A., (2015) 5 Medications that Cause Hearing
    Loss.   Retrieved

from:https://www.pharmacytimes.com/news/
5-medications-that-may-cause-hearing-loss

Hinkes, M (2009) Foothealth and amputation prevention for the long-term care resident. Retrieved from: https://www.mcknights.com/blogs/guest-columns/foot-health-and-amputation-prevention-for-the-long-term-care-resident/

Martin, K., Ham, E., Hilton, N. Z., (2018), Staff and Patient accounts of PRN medication administration and non-pharmacological interventions for anxiety. Retrieved from: https://pubmed.ncbi.nlm.nih.gov/29851211/ doi.org/10.1111/inm.2492

Thomas et al, (2014) Interventions to Reduce Inappropriate Prescribing of Antipsychotic Medications in People with Dementia Patient in Care Homes: A Systematic Review Journal of the American Medical Directors Association. Retrieved from: https://pubmed.ncbi.nlm.nih.gov/25112229/ DOI: 10.1016/j.jamda.2014.06.012

Vishnevsky, (2013) Senior dental care in facilities. Retrieved from: https://www.mcknights.com/marketplace/senior-dental-care-in-facilities/

CHAPTER EIGHT

Patient Safety

Learning Objectives

This section discusses in detail the steps to take for protection of the patient while addressing complaints or concerns, prevention of abuse, and plus, completing accident and incident reports.

Complaints or Concerns

ALTC center must develop a means of addressing complaints and concerns. These complaints can be brought to the attention of a facility representative by either a patient, family member, or staff. Complaints may vary from dislike of the food to any unpleasant treatment by a staff member. The action taken after a complaint is communicated is significant. Addressing these concerns should never be put off for another shift but handled immediately by the individual in charge. Reader, Gillespie, & Roberts (2014) discuss the benefits of patient complaints in a health care system. These are essential in improving the care and experience of patients. Each complaint should be carefully documented, and a thorough investigation ensue and resolved in a timely manner. The nursing staff must maintain communication with the patient and family at each stage in resolving the problem. The DON and LHA should be kept abreast of these complaints. Managing these challenges quickly exemplifies excellent customer service and allows the center to remain in compliance with the State and Federal Government. CMS conveys that complaints are the prevention of "abuse, neglect, exploitation and inadequate care or supervision". (CMS, 2017). Addressing complaints promptly and effectively is important for maintaining good customer service and meeting regulatory standards. To do so, it is necessary to thoroughly investigate the issue by interviewing the patient and relevant staff members, gathering statements, identifying the root cause of the problem, and proposing a solution for prevention in the future. Ignoring or delaying the resolution of complaints can lead to further dissatisfaction and potentially even regulatory violations. A patient may express dissatisfaction with a meal they received as an illustration. According to the state guidelines, a staff member must offer an alternative or something they would enjoy eating within their dietary restrictions. Further follow up would include the dietary department meeting with the patient and determining other nutritional food preferences and choices that could be made available at meal times. These concerns are certain to be looked at during the State Survey period, as well as any surprise visit from the Department of Public Health (DPH) from the state.

Documented legible logs of complaints and subsequent interventions implemented to resolve each problem is imperative for compliance with state regulations. Concerns will always arise but ignoring the patient concerns will only create greater problems with compliance and affect the patient satisfaction experience. Logging complaints and completing the paperwork required for investigations helps to prevent care abuse and maintain full center compliance.

Resident Council

The Resident Council is a right that must be honored by each facility. This meeting is privately held with members of the residents group population and is closed to staff members or visitors to the center. The residents can invite outsiders such as a staff member, family, friends or the state ombudsman, if they choose to do so. The meeting can be held monthly or quarterly as the residents choose. The center must accommodate the resident need for a private room and to send out notices timely for each meeting date. The center must also provide a staff member approved by the resident council, who will assist the members, take minutes and report their concerns to the Center Administrator. The center has a responsibility to respond timely with the action taken and give an explanation for the response.

Prevention of Abuse

Abuse is defined as neglect, exploitation, or willful harm to a patient. Different types of abuse include physical, mental, verbal, sexual, misappropriation of property, isolation because of behavior, or neglect. The Nursing Home Reform Act of 1987 focused on preventing abuse in the LTC setting. Prevention of abuse starts on the day of hire; a great portion of the prevention of abuse starts with hiring candidates with a background void of any history of abuse or criminal activity. (SOM, 2017). The State Operations Manual gives clear instructions on preventing abuse from occurring; it involves investigating any employee mentioned in a complaint of abuse. Any employee under investigation must be temporarily removed from interaction with the patient who brought the complaint until a full inquiry is finalized. The employee returns to patient care after the investigation has proven that there is no evidence of abuse. Records must be made available for proof of training with updated policies and procedures for the prevention of abuse. The Elder Justice Act (EJA) was formed to prevent elderly abuse when the Affordable Care Act was enacted (Dong, 2014). Any alleged abuse must be reported to all appropriate authorities in a very timely manner as required by the EJA. Depending upon severity, the alleged abuse is reported within the timely span of two hours from the occurrence. A thorough investigation begins immediately and reporting of the incident is not delayed until the probe is complete. If not reported in a timely manner, fines up to $200,000 can result. It is momentous to perform quick, thorough, and timely follow-up and execute appropriate interventions to prevent reoccurrence. Evidence of the complete documented investigation must be readily available to surveyors during the survey period.

Accident and Incident Reports

CMS, (2006) requires that a LTC center chronicle all accident and incident (A & I), of both known and unknown origins. The center is responsible for documenting all A & I report and are to be released upon request by state surveyors. A comprehensive investigation of an incident is completed by conducting interviews and follow through with statements and clear documentation of how the incident occurred, this is to be followed by a corrective action to prevent further incidents from occurring. Once the problem is identified, the patient must continue to be monitored; to verify the effectiveness of the intervention and ultimately achieve the goal of patient safety. Frequency of the same incident, on the same shift, with the same staff member, warrants a root cause analysis (RCA). Performing a RCA determines the systems that require modification to avert repeated incidences. Depending on the severity of an incident, it must be reported timely in accordance with the state's standard for reporting (Institute of Medicine, 2000). To foster compliance, A&I's should be completed soon after occurring, especially while the accident or incident is fresh in everyone's mind. The severity of each incident determines the reporting sequence. Alleged abuses are reported promptly to the Department of Public Health (DPH). Each state provides clear explanations and direction for reporting, from minor to major accidents and incidents. Each incident is logged chronologically by date and time, with the patient's name, room number, description of the incident and intervention implemented. A system organized with chronicling by year, month, and number, will enable a quick retrieval.

Falls with injuries, complaints of abuse and neglect are very serious; therefore, the staff in charge has a compulsory responsibility legally to notify the DON and LHA immediately to ensure timely reporting. A&I 's are time consuming due to lengthy investigations and, ensuring all documentation are completed, this includes witness statements, nursing notes, assessments, physician and family notification and interventions executed as planned. This lengthy, process can be the bane of a DON's existence, but the best practice option is for the nursing staff to avoid incomplete A&I's and for all nursing documentation, and other patient care paperwork turned in timely. Inquiry by a surveyor for an A & I may occur when a chart audit occurs and reveals documentation regarding incidents of a fall, a skin tear, a bruise or any unknown injury. Careful follow through, and documentation at the immediate time of the incident allows for a seamless survey experience.

Pressure Ulcer Prevention

Pressure ulcers are wounds that develop from unrelieved pressure applied to bony prominences; or other areas of the skin, which are repeatedly exposed to pressure resulting from lack of movement in that part of the body. Patients who are prone to developing pressure ulcers are either immobile or have multiple co-morbidities and underlying health factors. Every attempt must be made to prevent occurrences and any reoccurrences of pressure sores previously healed. One of the major aims of any LTC center is to prevent skin breakdown; an avoidable incident. Pressure ulcers are a significant financial burden, as they can lead to extended care stays and negatively impact quality indicators for long-term care centers. They are a major concern for CMS due to their costly nature and potential impact on patient outcomes. The SOM details how a facility should manage pressure ulcers. Increase in pressure ulcers are usually correlated to the quality of care received by patients.

Lyder and Ayello, (2008) stated in 2004, there were 455,000 hospital admissions related to pressure ulcers; each inpatient stay had a median cost of over $37,000. Efficacious systems in place beforehand can help prevent skin alteration. A critical component on admission is a thorough skin assessment performed within the first two hours of admission. On admission, the admitting nurse gathers data, and records all skin alterations with documentation of size, color, depth and the description with reference to any drainage or signs of infection. Based on the findings the nurse then communicates to the MD and gets the appropriate treatment. If the patient's skin assessment was not completed in a timely manner and subsequently develops a pressure ulcer, the LTC center could potentially be held liable for an acquired pressure ulcer. Preventing pressure ulcers are not only important but also quite significant to consider the impact on patients with preexisting skin disorders. Improving admissions for these patients can be a key focus when it comes to preventing pressure ulcers and improving overall patient outcomes. Another consideration to prevent pressure ulcers in the LTC setting is that the nursing staff must focus on identifying patients prone to developing pressure ulcers first and implement the appropriate treatments, nutrition, protective equipment, and surveillance ahead of time. Increased shearing, friction, moisture from incontinence, and immobility can all contribute to pressure sores. Minimizing these central elements helps in preventing skin deteriorations. Most LTC centers have implemented the Braden or Norton scale to determine those at substantial risk for pressure ulcers. Lyder and Ayello (2008) noted the benefits of implementing a pressure ulcer prevention program. They also explore programs that simultaneously prevent pressure ulcers and reduce costs. Depending on the LTC census size, an Infection Prevention Nurse/Wound Care Nurse (IPN/WCN) controls this department and reports to the DON on a weekly basis. The IPN/WCN leads the wound surveillance program that oversees monitoring of wounds on a daily basis with measurement of each wound with documentation of progress in healing. A WCN must be able to assess and determine the difference stages of a wound, differentiating the different types of wounds, as well as identify a Deep Tissue Injury (DTI) or an unstageable wound.

They are also responsible for post healing skin monitoring. Surveyors will customarily request wound progress documentation, especially if there is a negative trend and above the acceptable wound rate for the national and state acceptable average. A successful surveillance program has a provider responsible for providing supporting documentation carried out by the designated RN or the IPN. An excellent pressure ulcer prevention system includes the documentation of weekly assessments of skin including: measurements showing, improvement or decline, and continued wound surveillance, post healing. The program must include ways of monitoring for adequate nutritional daily intake and interventions for improvement. The CNA Care Card and instruction should include; turning and repositioning for those vulnerable patients, consequently preventing a patient from staying in one position, specifically sitting in a chair or lying in bed for long periods of time. Daily directions and protocols should also involve keeping the patient's skin clean and dry, as well as, report any changes immediately to the charge nurse. Slow and non-healing wounds compel assessing the root cause and additional interventions to prevent further deterioration. From personal experience I have observed an outside entity run by wound care physicians, they make weekly wound rounds in LTC centers, and care for these wounds till healed. A wound consultant physician who specializes in chronic wounds may help a LTC center improve their chronic wounds cases. Takashini et al, (2008) emphasizes the significance of recognizing the different types of wound and caring for them appropriately. They also describe the treatment for pressure ulcers, venous ulcers, neuropathic, and ischemic ulcers. A specialized wound consultant can distinguish different wound types and conditions, as well as, document changes appropriately. During a survey process the surveyors will also view orders, verify any recommendations were carried out, and look at any decline in a patient's health status. Included in their inquiry is also verifying that treatment modalities were done efficiently and in a timely manner. If a survey investigation reveals missing documentation or any discrepancies, neglect or patient harm, a citation, deficiency or fine will be imposed.

Pressure Relieving Equipment

One of the most effective means of preventing pressure ulcers is the use of pressure relieving surface mattresses, and cushions. An effective wound prevention program identifies those at risk for developing a pressure ulcer immediately on admission and to quickly coordinate the necessary supplies and equipment needed to focus on protecting the bony prominences such as heels, knees, hips, elbows, coccyx, and posterior head. These areas are the most vulnerable and the most important focus areas for prevention. There are different kinds of mattresses used in this setting for immobile patients, Low Air Loss (LAL) mattresses, Alternating Pressure Mattresses (APM), Clinitron bed, foam mattresses and others can also be used. Pressure relieving mattresses can be ineffective if the incorrect setting is utilized. The setting on a pressure-relieving mattress refers to the specific adjustment of the mattress that is used to provide support and comfort to the patient. The settings can be set for comfort and also set for a specific weight range. For example, if the patient's weight is set incorrectly, the mattress would possibly become too hard, and no pressure is relieved subsequently a wound could potentially develop or deteriorate. Standard monitoring involves checking to make sure the mattress is set correctly for the patient's needs. If a problem is identified and the mattress is defective in providing the necessary protection, it should be immediately addressed and resolved to the extent of replacing with a new mattress. When a patient has a wound and the settings are for comfort but set incorrectly to extra firm, the surface then becomes similar to a hard surface causing unrelieved pressure for a wound to decline or a new pressure area to develop. Increasing pressure ulcers in a LTC facility reflects negatively; therefore, a LTC center should implement systems to prevent these wounds from ever happening in the first place. Patients with wounds are generally evaluated and investigated to assure all preventative measures are in place. A surveyor may check a patient's bed, observe the mattress setting, view records, check for documentation revealing frequent monitoring, and confirm that all the settings are correct. Care plans need to reflect the type of specialty mattress for each patient, with an order in place, including, the specific setting for each patient. This should be monitored each shift by the nursing staff and the responsibility should not be delegated to any non-licensed staff member. The ultimate goal is patient safety and protection. Structures to prevent pressure ulcers and monitoring of the guidance systems will assist in accomplishing patient safety objectives.

Prevention of the Spread of Infection

Prevention of infection is a fundamental part of the nurse's role in all LTC facilities. Each center must develop an Infection Control Program to monitor, document, and prevent the spread of infections. This program monitors antibiotic usage, as well as, any occurrence of UTI Pneumonia (PNA), Upper and Lower Respiratory Infections (URI and LRI), Multi Drug Resistant Organisms (MDRO), and Wound Infections. Smith, et al (2008) suggest that Pneumonia is one of the leading causes of illness in a LTC setting and is preventable. Outbreaks of infection are reported according to the state and federal requirements. A state operator's manual (SOM) contains specific instruction to guide the program. The Infection Control Program must provide record keeping for Infection Control reporting and staff training. These include: effective handwashing, surveillance, immunization program including influenza for both employees and patients. An effective immunization program can help prevent this from happening. CMS, (2009) indicates the requirement for an Infection Control Program includes investigating all infections, properly protecting patients by cohorting as appropriate or implementing precautionary measures, careful documentation, plan for interventions and results of each intervention. Each LTC facility may vary in which staff member oversees the Infection Control Department. Some may hire a Registered Nurse (RN), Licensed Practical Nurse (LPN), or a Licensed Vocational Nurse (LVN) with an RN oversite to fulfill the state infection control regulations and standards. Effective November 2019 the nurse in charge must be qualified and certified in Infection Prevention practices. Tuberculosis (TB) surveillance is done for both employees and patients. Infection control programs must perform surveillance of all facility and community acquired infections, and regularly scheduled infection control surveillance rounds on all units. The IPN assures that regulatory standards are used in treatment and infections reported meet McGeers criteria (CMS, 2009). Another very important task is also to monitor the environment, checking for potential outbreaks of upper respiratory infections; influenza, colds, respiratory syncytial virus, norovirus, adenovirus, or the new Corona Virus

(COVID-19). These infections can potentially be introduced by both visitors and employees, during seasons of increased infections. Signs should be posted throughout the facility instructing visitors to not visit if they are sick. Patients with infections are to be quarantined if an outbreak does occur. Calculation of the percentage of compromised patients determine the necessity to temporarily halt admissions in a center in order to prevent an epidemic. Employees should be diligent in maintaining their health and avoid coming to work while feeling ill to prevent the transmission of infections to the patients. Some Gastrointestinal (GI) infections are highly contagious and should be monitored carefully, an example is Clostridium-Difficile(C-Diff). These C-diff spores are resilient and stay on surfaces or inanimate objects, such as, bed rails, door knobs, and other surfaces for a very long time; for this reason, all surfaces must be cleaned and disinfected meticulously. The IPN makes sure the appropriate cleaning solutions are used to eliminate these spores, while policies and procedures (P&P) should indicate how to handle these types of organisms. After a patient is discharged from an isolation room, the room and all its equipment must be cleaned and sanitized before the next patient is admitted to that room. Applying McGeers criteria, provides the benchmark for determining if an illness is a true infection. Hand hygiene is the most important means of preventing infection spreading between patients. Hand sanitizers should be available for quick hand sanitizing of unsoiled hands and, if soiled, use soap and water applying friction with both hands to remove any residue from the hands. Frequent hand hygiene audits aid in monitoring staff compliance with infection prevention. Ultimately, hand hygiene is the responsibility of all staff members.

Prevalence of Indwelling Catheters

Indwelling catheters are a necessity when used in conditions when a patient is unable to void or in cases where a decubitus wound needs to be protected from bodily secretions. In a LTC center, indwelling catheters are only used in appropriate circumstances, such as for the correct diagnosis and pertinent medical condition, and their use is carefully documented for necessity. It is unacceptable to place an indwelling catheter for convenience of incontinence or even a single diagnosis. According to CMS, a patient admitted to a center without an indwelling catheter must not be catheterized except for medical necessity. Similarly, a patient who is admitted to a STR center with an indwelling catheter must be assessed and the indwelling catheter removed when medically cleared (CMS, 2017). Appropriateness for an indwelling catheter, involves the correct diagnosis which includes Obstructive Uropathy or Neurogenic bladder with another diagnosis such as stage III or stage IV wound, or some type of terminal illness. A voiding trial is performed by a urologist and if the patient fails the voiding trial, documentation must exist that notes the correct diagnosis documented by the physician in the chart with the physician's order for the catheter to remain. Care planning, monitoring and documenting the patient's tolerance is important. Assessment of any discomfort and abnormality is reported to the patient's physician and monitoring of the output, odor, color and any sediments are very important. Scheduled changes of the indwelling catheter must be performed periodically at least every thirty days and as needed to prevent infections. According to Smith, et al, (2008) indwelling catheters are likely to contract infections and are a significant source of microbes. Not only should indwelling catheters be monitored and used appropriately; but, best practices in healthcare are to prevent indwelling catheter associated infections.

Alarms

Alarms are used to alert staff members when an at-risk patient attempts to independently move in bed, chair. An alarm notification may occur while a fall is taking place or attempts to get up from their position. Other alarms used are motion sensors that sound on movement if the patient is in the vicinity of the sensor. They also are available as pad alarms, bed and chair pad alarms that activate when pressure is lifted in a chair or bed. Alarms are frequently used as an intervention to alert the staff that a patient is up and possibly intercept before a fall occurs. However, many such alarms have proven ineffective in preventing serious falls. An alarm used alone as an intervention has shown to be late in notifying the staff. When an alarm sounds, often the patient has already fallen. Ogundo, (2016) suggest that frequent rounding by the nursing staff, should include assisting patients with simple tasks such as toileting and reaching for personal items, and noting the last time a patient was seen. He also notes rounding can be a more effective alternative to alarms intercepting falls. Not only are alarms ineffective at best in preventing falls, they disturb a patient's sleep. This is especially true for a cognitively challenged patient. A fall may also occur in an attempt to eliminate the aggravation from a nearby alarm. As the DON directs the daily routine, fall prevention and injuries are high priority to keep patients safe. From personal knowledge, some facilities have become alarm free centers introducing hourly rounding as an effective intervention instead of alarms.

Fall Prevention and Safety

Each center requires a fall prevention program that identifies fall risks for each patient to put an individualized fall prevention care plan in place.

Preventing falls begins with implementing a solid fall risk program. On admission, an assessment of each patient for fall risk identifies those in need of additional fall prevention interventions. A CNA Care Card is updated with the individual care needs in regards to fall risk, transfer status and assistance needed. A patient potentially may fall due to balancing issues, delayed toileting needs, confusion or anxiety, especially those newly admitted and unfamiliar with their surroundings. Schneider & Beattie, (2014) refer to falls as a major cause in adult injuries. They mention that approximately every 30 minutes someone dies from a fall related injury. Close monitoring of fall prevention techniques and continual observation of safety concerns when rounding is pivotal for each shift. Staff should also observe for slippery floors, exposed wiring, tubing, or cords that may pose a hazard to all patients. Assuring that all patient care items are in proximity will prevent a fall in an attempt by the patient to reach the needed items, losing their balance and subsequently sustain a fall. A good fall prevention program keeps track of the number of falls, the times and shifts that the falls occur, the physical and mental status at the time of fall, activities before the fall, whether the fall was witnessed, and if interventions were put in place for fall prevention. Some falls may not be preventable, the priority should always be to prevent any injuries from happening. Those with frequent falls are discussed at an interdisciplinary fall risk meeting and recommendations made for each patient safety to decrease falls. A route cause analysis (RCA) essentially establishes the reason for the fall and putting effective interventions into place to prevent future falls. Preventing falls can decrease the rising cost of healthcare, Schneider & Beattie, (2014) discuss that patients transferred to a hospital specifically for falls cost billions annually. Early identification of patients who are at risk for fall and applying appropriate interventions immediately upon admission will assist in decreasing the number of falls. A comprehensive fall risk program should include a variety of measures to help prevent falls and ensure the safety of patients. High fall risk patients can be readily identified by placing signs outside the doorways of their room on each unit. To ensure that these signs are easily understood and compliant with HIPAA regulations, they should be prominently displayed and use clear, recognizable symbols such as a falling leaf, a falling star, or a falling plane without any identifying personal information.

In addition to these signs, it may also be helpful to have a system in place for alerting staff members to the presence of high fall risk patients, such as using special wristbands or other forms of identification. Other strategies that can be included in a fall risk program include the use of bed and chair alarms, the implementation of fall prevention protocols, and the provision of additional assistance to patients as needed. By taking a comprehensive approach to fall prevention, the healthcare facilities can help ensure the safety and well-being of their patients, and improve the patient experience as well as, affecting healthcare costs. Initiating a fall risk care plan, includes accommodating any special assistance needed; primarily, toileting needs and transferring assistance. A CNA Care Card details the transfer level of the patient and their fall risk status together with hourly rounding each shift on the patients. Monitoring patient safety is paramount for fall prevention

Restraints

Restraints are prohibited by state regulations but vary by each state and are to be utilized according to a medical necessity. They cannot be used for ease of benefit to the facility or punishment to a patient. The State Operations Manual (SOM) also notes that freedom of movement should not be inhibited by use of restraints (SOM, 2017). While restraints such as side rails, seat belts, lap trays and lap tables, can help prevent falls, they can also contribute to injury if not used properly. A thorough evaluation considering the potential risks and benefits must be done before assigning a particular restraint to a patient. The individual care plan must reflect the assignment, with direction to check the status of the restraint every two hours while in use, to prevent any harm to the patient. CMS, (2017) directs that all LTC facilities must limit the usage of restraints for the prevention of falls. It also indicates that there is more evidence that shows, harm from use of restraints. More than two side rails are considered a restraint, a patient can potentially get trapped between the bed rails in an attempt to exit a bed and cause a confused patient to sustain an injury. Seat belts prevent a patient's mobility, which in turn inhibits them from rising and sitting freely. Potentially, pressure ulcers can develop from sitting too long Some facilities have chosen to forbid the use of restraints, especially stopping the use of alarmed seat belts attached to wheelchairs. Orders for monitoring should specify frequency of nursing documentation; therefore, proving frequent observation, frequent toileting, and frequent ambulation. At times a confused patient may require an intervention of mitts to prevent dislocation of an Intravenous (IV) line after multiple replacements.

The SOM requires that when a restraint is used for absolute medical necessity, the duration of use should be a short timeframe with documentation of frequent monitoring. Mohler, Richter, Kopke, and Meyer (2011) mention the adverse effects of restraints and note that patients can be affected psychologically, and physically. During the annual survey proceedings, the use of restraints is scrutinized both for physical and pharmaceutical reasons. The main objective is to enable each patient to reach their highest potential capability and, if restraints are utilized, the patient's safety care is of utmost importance.

Nutrition and Weight Management

Nutrition and weight loss are a significant element for a patient in the LTC setting. During a center's survey, the importance and scrutiny of these areas are emphasized. This data also available for public view on the five-star rating system for all centers. The DON in collaboration with the Registered Dietician (RD) is responsible for developing systems and plans to prevent patient weight loss and/or decline in nutritional status. Litchford, Dorner, & Posthauer, (2014) specify the important role of the RD who coordinates with the interdisciplinary team to manage patient weight loss or unhealthy weight gains. The resident's weight monitoring begins with obtaining an initial weight on the day of admission, along with gathering data such as their health status, ability to eat, consistency of foods eaten, and the appropriate diet to improve and sustain the patient's health status. Based on this information, an individualized care plan is formulated. A patient may be admitted with "failure to thrive" or a poor appetite putting them at greater risk for weight loss and decline. While in the LTC center, every effort must be made and documented to prevent a patient's further decline. A diagnosis of Congestive Heart Failure (CHF) requires frequent weight monitoring which is daily and reporting changes in weight to the provider immediately.

Those at risk for weight loss, are weighed more frequently, while a more stable patient can be monitored less often like weekly. A system must be in place that directs the nursing staff to monitor weights closely and allows the provider to make the appropriate adjustments as necessary. Strict monitoring will prevent any unexpected weight changes and allow timely prevention of undesirable weight loss or weight gain. A poor appetite can lead to weight loss, which in turn may negatively lead to other health problems.

Such a decline in nutritional status could potentially develop into a pressure ulcer if not addressed early. The nursing leadership staff makes sure these critical areas are surveilled to prevent weight related problems. Monitoring patient weights involves coordinating staffing, possessing an accurate calibrated scale, documenting the correct weight and reporting any changes appropriately. Residents should be closely monitored by a registered nurse, who should report any findings or changes to the medical doctor or nurse practitioner and obtain orders for necessary interventions. A patient's significant weight loss should prompt an investigation and inquiry into the reason for the weight loss while considering factors such as, percentage of meals eaten, nutritional status and a review of medications that may alter the patient's appetite. The nursing staff should also verify whether preferences or choices are offered at meal times to the patient and if assistance is needed or the appropriate utensils are being used. It is also very important to consider dentition, especially, those who are communicatively challenged, checking for cavities, or other dental issues such as ill fitted dentures. Poorly fitting dentures are sure signs that a patient is not able to consume adequate portions at each meal because there might be pain with chewing or dentures shifting while chewing. Swallowing difficulties should be considered and at this juncture obtain a Speech Pathologist consult. With the implementation of the electronic record, necessary data mining allows reports to view trends in weight loss, meal and fluid percentages that can help make decisions in adjustments and projections. Weight loss can be a warning sign of poor care for patients and is included in the five-star rating system for healthcare centers provided by the Center for Medicare Services (CMS). Care must be person centered, allowing each patient to reach or maintain their highest practical level of performance. Proactive care includes consultation with a RD for triggers, that may cause weight loss, poor appetite, weight gain and discussion of resident meal preferences.

Despite the appropriate interventions, weight loss may be inevitable with relation to a terminally ill patient. In this patient's condition, documentation, orders and care planning needs must mirror the patient's status in the medical record. A hospice patient or terminally ill patient will eventually lose weight from a poor appetite. It is important for documentation and follow through by the physician with the terminal diagnosis, and reasons why a decline in weight and health is expected and/or inevitable. The physician can order the appropriate level of care if there are no improvement in health status. A thorough nursing assessment captures patients on a decline or those experiencing weight loss. Litchford, Dorner, & Posthauer, (2014) note that functional assessments can determine nutritional status. Low pre-albumin levels can also determine a patient's nutritional status. However, the writers disagree that a lab draw of pre-albumin is an accurate means of determining nutritional status; whatever system or measurement tool used to determine nutritional declines, needs to be consistent. Patient records should indicate data gathered and interventions implemented along with improvements and the desired outcomes. If the desired outcome is not achieved, a disciplinary team meeting is necessary including recommendations for other treatment. Weight loss is viewed by the state surveyors carefully during survey for deviation from state standards. Failure to monitor or make appropriate adjustments in the care plan in the cases of weight loss, or a failure to identify a patient who has had significant weight loss, can result in harm and subsequently fines or citations. This is significant and can potentially affect a patient's level of activity and ability to perform ADL's. The patient's nutrition status is pertinent for energy and the ability to accomplish necessary and intense therapy and/or rehabilitation to return to baseline health status.

<u>*Resources*</u>

CMS, (2006), State Operators Manual: Retrieved from: https://www.cms.gov/Regulations-and-Guidance/Guidance/Transmittals/downloads/R21SOMA.pdf

CMS, (2009), Infection Control, Retrieved from: https://www.cms.gov/Regulations-and-Guidance/Guidance/Transmittals/downloads/r51soma.pdf, Infection Control

CMS, (2017) State Operations Manual, Retrieved from: https://www.cms.gov/Regulations-and-Guidance/Guidance/Manuals/Downloads/som107c05.pdf

CMS, (2017) State Operations Manual, Long term Care Facility, Retrieved from: https://www.cms.gov/Regulations-and-Guidance/Guidance/Manuals/downloads/som107ap_pp_guidelines_ltcf.pdf

Dong, X. (2014). Elder Abuse: Research, Practice, and Health Policy. The 2012 GSA Maxwell Pollack

Award Lecture. *The Gerontologist*, *54*(2), 153–162. http://doi.org/10.1093/geront/gnt139

Institute of Medicine, (2000). Committee on Quality of Health Care in America; Kohn LT, Corrigan JM, Donaldson MS, editors. To Err is Human: Building a Safer Health System. Washington (DC): National Academies Press (US); 2000. D, Characteristics of State Adverse Event Reporting Systems. Available from: https://www.ncbi.nlm.nih.gov/books/NBK225168/

Lyder C.H., Ayello E.A. (2008), Pressure Ulcers: A Patient Safety Issue. In: Hughes RG, editor. Patient Safety and Quality: An Evidence-Based Handbook for Nurses. Rockville (MD): Agency for Healthcare Research and Quality (US); 2008 Apr. Chapter 12 Available from: https://www.ncbi.nlm.nih.gov/books/NBK2650

Litchford, M. D., Dorner, B., & Posthauer, M. E. (2014). Malnutrition as a Precursor of Pressure

Ulcers. *Advances in Wound Care, 3*(1), 54–63. http://doi.org/10.1089/wound.2012.0385

Mohler, R., Richter, T., Kopke, S. Meyer, G., (2011) Interventions for Preventing and Reducing the Use of Physical Restraints in Long-Term Geriatric Care. Cochrane Database of Systematic Reviews Issue 2. Art. No.: CD007546. DOI:10.1002/14651858.CD007546.pub2

Ogundu, O U., (2016), "Fall Reduction among Elderly Residents in Skilled Nursing Facility." *All Regis University Theses.* 731. Retrieved from: https://epublications.regis.edu/theses/731

Schneider, E. C., & Beattie, B. L. (2014). Building the Older Adult Fall Prevention Movement – Steps and Lessons Learned. *Frontiers in Public Health, 2,* 194. http://doi.org/10.3389/fpubh.2014.00194

Smith, P. W., Bennett, G., Bradley, S., Drinka, P., Lautenbach, E., Marx, J., ... Stevenson, K. (2008). SHEA/APIC Guideline: Infection

Prevention and Control in the Long-Term Care Facility. *Infection Control and Hospital Epidemiology*, *29*(9), 785–814. http://doi.org/10.1086/592416

Reader, T. W., Gillespie, A., & Roberts, J. (2014). Patient complaints in healthcare systems: a systematic review and coding taxonomy. *BMJ Quality & Safety*, *23*(8), 678–689. http://doi.org/10.1136/bmjqs-2013-002437

Takahashi et al, (2007) Wound care technologies: Emerging evidence for appropriate use in Long-Term Care. Retrieved from: managed healthcareconnect.com

CHAPTER NINE

Center Meetings

Learning Objectives

In this chapter, you will learn about the different types of meetings that take place in a center. 1. Daily Team Meetings, 2. Discharge Team Meetings, 3. Quarterly Medical Staff Meetings, 4. Nursing Staff

Daily Team Meetings

At the start of the day each week, the Interdisciplinary team gathers to discuss individual patient specifics; such as, changes in condition, concerns, needs, interventions or patients at-risk. The meeting is interactive, and input is routinely contributed by all departments involved in patient care. Team members include physicians, nurses, therapy department, recreation, dietary, the Center Administrator, DON, ADON, Case Manager (CM) or Unit Manager (UM), Infection Prevention Nurse (IPN), Wound Care Nurse (WCN) and Staff Development Coordinator (SDC). Individual roles vary by center and all listed may not attend. Some centers also solicit input from other departments such as housekeeping, maintenance, and the admissions department in order to discuss and notify any problems or updates concerning their specific areas. Each nursing unit representative reports on patient changes in condition with dialogue of interventions and outcomes including follow up on significant issues put in place interventions discussed. The DON, LHA or

ADON conducts the team meeting and comments or queries actions or interventions made on patient care. The nursing management team at this meeting looks at possible areas lacking in safety and assures adequate patient care is maintained and also makes recommendations for appropriate follow up. These actions validate whether a change in condition was reported to the physician and whether the doctors' orders were carried out appropriately. The nurse following up will report back to the DON as the day progresses. Raine, Wallace, Nic a' Bháird, et al. (2014) emphasizes the importance and the effects of team meetings on the care of chronically ill patients. Discussion also takes place on discharges, census level, prospective admissions, and any other problems and concerns identified by the team members. The 24-hour report is frequently utilized and used to record the previous shift's activity along with any changes in condition specifically falls, skin tears, change in health status, new or current antibiotics as well as transfers in and out of the center and or anything that the DON deems significant for report each morning. There are additional meetings throughout the week scheduled as deemed necessary by the center, including the discharge team meeting.

Discharge Team Meetings

Plans for discharge originate on admission, a discharge planning meeting is held at least once or twice per week for all short-term patients admitted or LTC resident that needs to be transferred to another setting. This meeting facilitates discussion among the interdisciplinary team about the patient's progress. Any barriers and challenges to discharge are also addressed. Participants in the meeting are from each discipline; including Physical Therapy, Occupational Therapy Nursing, Social Services, Respiratory Therapy, Registered Dietician, and any other department considered appropriate, depending on the center specialty areas. Each interdisciplinary team member may discuss progress in recovery and suggest recommendations to the team to achieve the ultimate goal for a safe discharge for each patient. Behm & Grey, (nd) discuss the effectiveness of an interdisciplinary team in the care of a patient. According to the

Improving Medicare Post-Acute Care Transformation (IMPACT) Act of 2014, a discharge plan must be developed and communicated within the first 24 hours to the patient or responsible party. Discharge goals are based on the patient preference to carry out a patient centered care (CMS, 2015). Teaching for discharge begins on admission; for example, a newly diagnosed Diabetic needs education on how to monitor their disease, check their blood sugar, how to manage a low blood sugar, how to administer their own insulin and dietary recommendations to assist in keeping blood sugar levels at a reasonable level. A patient with a new colostomy may also need teaching on how to manage their appliance, change and empty the pouch, as well as, what to observe on their skin for abnormal changes. If a patient is incapable of understanding or performing return demonstration, a family member or caregiver is then given the responsibility and taught how to perform these tasks. Discussions at the meeting also address the patient's current ambulation status, ability to perform all activities of daily living (ADL's), and any nursing barriers or medical issues that may prevent a safe discharge. Patients that are unable to perform simple ADL's or require more assistance than family members can provide, may need 24hour care at home or at a qualified facility. Documentation regarding communication with a patient to be discharged must be made available and if the patient is incapable of functioning independently in the community, reasons for the decision and who made the decision for alternative care is also to be documented by the physician. Upon discharge, a patient receives a discharge summary, with history of stay, current medications, treatments and recommendations for follow-up in the community (SOM, 2016). Significant planning precedes a successful patient discharge. The discharge meeting ensures that accommodations can be met at home or an alternative setting. The patient is provided the appropriate durable medical equipment (DME) such as a walker, cane, wheelchair or raised toilet seat and a shower bench. Other supplies needed might be wound care supplies or tube feeding supplies and anything specifically for their discharge diagnosis. Follow up appointments are scheduled with any Primary Care Physician (PCP) or Specialist for continued care. Continuity of care may also require home care services for nursing, physical therapy or occupational therapy. Other patients specifically hemodialysis dialysis patients require arrangements made for medical transportation. All these efforts for a safe discharge to the next level of care. All parties associated for follow-up after discharge receives a copy of the discharge summary. This includes the following: The Primary Care Physician (PCP), any specialist that the patient will follow up with the patient, Homecare (HC), and the family member or caregiver responsible for that patient after discharge. Discharge records are secured with other records and can be requested by the surveyors during the annual survey process.

Quarterly Medical Staff Meetings

The Quarterly Medical Staff Meeting brings together all the covering Physicians, Pharmacist, Nurse Practitioner (NP), Physician's Assistant (PA) a Chaplin, if one is on staff, the Licensed Home Administrator (LHA), the Director of Nursing, (DON), the Assistant Director of Nursing, (ADON), the Staff Development Coordinator (SDC), the Infection Prevention Nurse

(IPN), the Wound Care Nurse, (WCN), Director of Rehabilitation, and an Administrative Assistant. The meeting is presided over by the LHA and DON and called to order and confirmed by two attendees. Those present must sign in to complete the record of attendance. The LTC Administrator further discusses in detail the Quality Assurance and Performance Improvement (QAPI), as well as any advancement and developments occurring or plans in the future for changes and improvements. At this assembly center progress is discussed, such as, patient falls specifically addressed including: number of falls, total falls with or without injuries, the number of times the falls occur and reason the patient fell with discussion of all interventions put in place. The quarterly medical staff meeting also discusses the total amount of deaths that occurred in the previous quarter and if those were anticipated deaths. The IPN discusses specifications on infection control while focusing on infections that were communicable such as pneumonia, Multi Drug Resistant Organisms (MDRO), upper and lower respiratory infections, influenza. Other discussion also elaborates on wounds and wound infections rate as well UTI's. Center census is reported with the current 5-star rating and suggestions for improvements where necessary. Other areas include rates of re-admission to the hospital and ways to enhance improvement of readmission rates. Survey readiness is always a topic of discussion whether the survey window has passed or the survey window is steadily approaching since preparation for survey involves all the team members. Assigned personnel will record the exchanges amongst the team and prepare minutes for the next quarterly meeting.

Nursing Staff Meetings

Nursing staff meetings are an integral part of the nursing department where they address problems, and provide information about new changes from the LTC center, organization, state, and federal levels. Information must be disseminated quickly since changes occur frequently in any center, organization, or industry. It is imperative that any communication regarding updates and revisions in a center's policies or communication of problems to be addressed and any immediate change necessary is done in a professional and timely manner. Some information can be communicated through email or newsletters, but in person meetings require gathering of staff members in a 24-hour setting. Ensuring that there is adequate nursing coverage to provide care on each nursing unit is crucial to facilitate face to face meetings. Holding frequent but short meetings to inform nursing personnel of any changes, lessens the after effect of information overload at one lengthy session. The DON or LHA must consider staffing hours, nursing schedules, and overtime, in order to schedule these meetings. Conducting a staff meeting just before the end or the middle of a shift allows the nursing staff to plan and organize their day. Meetings should not only discuss problems and updates but also utilize the opportunity to commend the staff on a job well done. Using an organized, attractive handout for in-services, email, or newsletter along with follow-up help get important information disseminated quickly.

At-Risk Meetings

At-risk meetings are critical in a center and serves to identify patients vulnerable for falls, pressure ulcers, dehydration, nutrition risk factors and weight loss or weight gain. They are usually discussed at the daily interdisciplinary meetings but more in-depth discussion for interventions are needed at this specific meeting. Significant positive outcomes are seen when susceptible patients are identified and monitored more closely to prevent any further and major decline. When a patient is admitted and determined to have potential for weight changes, they are followed more closely. This is done through interventions, such as, weight monitoring, dietician consultation, and reporting changes to the physician in a timely manner. Subsequent interventions are evaluated for effectiveness with any changes made as appropriate. The same applies to those at-risk for skin alteration. The Nursing staff ensure that appropriate equipment is available for patients, such as, pressure relieving mattresses or beds, wound therapy supplies, nutrition support from the RD and coordination with the physician. The at-risk meetings provide a platform for overseeing the effectiveness of interventions on these vulnerable patients. Close and consistent observation is performed to prevent a decline; resulting in a positive outcome for the patient. Vogelsmeier, (2011) comments on the positive impact that a facility's nursing team can have on patients when monitoring specific areas of concerns. The DON may direct the at-risk meetings but they can also be delegated appropriately to a qualified and experienced RN. These meetings should include: the DON, ADON, IPN, Unit Managers (UM) or Case Managers (CM), Nursing Supervisors and a Medical Provider which varies from center to center. Meetings should be documented with details about the discussions related to each patient, including any interventions, outcomes, and changes that were discussed, plans for follow up as well as the names of the attendees. These reports must be made available should it be requested by surveyors at any times.

Resources

Behm & Grey, (nd) Interdisciplinary Rehabilitation Team; Retrieved from: http://samples.jbpub.com/9781449634476/80593_ch05_5806.pdf

CMS, (2015), Hospital Acquired Conditions, retrieved from: https://www.cms.gov/medicare/medicare-fee-for-service-payment/hospitalacqcond/hospital-acquired_conditions.html

Raine R, Wallace I, Nic a' Bháird C, et al. (2014) Improving the effectiveness of multidisciplinary team meetings for Patients with chronic diseases: a prospective observational study. Southampton (UK): NIHR Journals Library; (Health Services and Delivery Research, No. 2.37.) Scientific summary. Retrieved from: https://www.ncbi.nlm.nih.gov/books/NBK260202/

State Operations Manual, (2016). Retrieved from: http://www.hpm.umn.edu/nhregsplus/Resour ces%20and%20Publications/CMS_Survey_Re sources/CMS/Appx_SOM_483.30%20-%20Nursing%20Services.pdf

Vogelsmeier, A. A., (2011) The safety and quality of long-term care. Retrieved from: https://psnet.ahrq.gov/webmm/case/248/the-safety-and-quality-of-long-term-care

CHAPTER TEN

Transfers

Learning Objectives

In this chapter, discussion will elaborate on the processes for resident transfers and bed-hold policies.

Emergent Transfers

The need for the management of an acute change in condition necessitates a transfer to a higher level of care, especially in life threatening conditions. Prudence in pinpointing signs and symptoms early and addressing them promptly may prevent some emergent transfers. CMS, (2010) enacted laws where payment for patients re-admitted to the hospital with the same diagnoses, within a 30-day period, is withheld. These include conditions such as, Urinary Tract Infections (UTI), as well as surgical site infections and since the enactment many other conditions were added to the list. CMS, (2015) explained that the rulings in 2008 identified diagnoses that were preventable and costly in the acute care setting; therefore, should not be reimbursed for subsequent reoccurrences. Now included in this ruling are LTC centers receiving reimbursement from Medicare and Medicaid. This now requires meticulous follow-through by the nursing staff, starting from admissions to discharge. This is done by identifying potential problems by careful monitoring of patients each shift, promptly identifying and addressing symptoms or complaints before becoming unmanageable. Ouslander, (2014) describes the development of the INTERACT program, which is abbreviated for "Interventions to Reduce Acute Care Transfers". The INTERACT forms are completed upon any patient transfer to an acute care setting. The nursing staff reports to a clinician in the ED giving details of the reason for the transfer, detailing interventions that were executed before the transfer, and the outcome or response from such treatments. Copies of the same INTERACT forms are also to be given to the responding Emergency Medical Technicians (EMT), where a copy is sent to the ED, and a copy is also kept for the patient records. More importantly, INTERACT has provided pathways to monitor patients and identify any changes in their condition early. The premise is to treat a condition early before the need for a transfer to an acute care setting arises. The end objective of the INTERACT is a reduction in unnecessary costs and improvement in the quality of care. The INTERACT form describes treatment or special services provided by the transferring center and is completed on every emergent transfer. Emergent transfers are carefully tracked by CMS, patients that return to the hospital within 30 days after being admitted with the same diagnoses may result in the acute care hospital being unpaid for those services. Previously, only acute care hospitals were penalized for 30-day readmissions. This has now been extended to LTC, STR and Home Care facilities as part of the Affordable Care Act (ACA) in 2010. This change was done to enhance patient care and reduce healthcare costs (Bartels, Gill, & Naslund, 2015). It provides an opportunity for LTC and STR nurses to increase their clinical assessment skills and critical thinking ability, to identify key signs and symptoms, address the problems early and achieve the primary goal for preventing an unnecessary emergent transfer.

Patients are generally transferred for management of acute symptoms. Warning signs recognized early can prevent a medical condition from escalating into an unmanageable status. Bartel, Gill & Naslund, (2015) stated that Accountable Care

Organizations (ACO) were formed from the ACA and they work towards managing healthcare costs and delivering a high quality of patient care. Providers of external care facilities such as Home Care Agencies, LTC and STR facilities, Medical Groups and hospitals are all combined to form an ACO. Preference for admission is given to facilities that have implemented the INTERACT form and keep their re-admission rates at a reasonably low rate. ACO meetings are held frequently and centers must maintain an acceptable standard on issues mentioned above in order to remain in the ACO. The population of patients transferring to and from an acute care setting varies. It is highly important that transfers within the center are appropriate; therefore, transfers should be done so there is no psychosocial effect on the patient. When a transfer occurs, all parties must be informed and documented in the chart to prove the patient had the opportunity to refuse the transfer (Elizaitis, 2020).

Bed-hold Policy

LTC and STR facilities licensed to accept Medicaid patients, are required to have a bed-hold for a temporary period for those transferred out to an acute care setting. Bed-hold policies are upheld by the state and must be issued to patients upon transfer to an acute care setting. Medicaid will pay a facility to reserve a patient's bed for return, up to a certain period. Unruh et al (2013) indicates that the facility must have a minimum occupancy rate to be reimbursed for bed-holds. From firsthand experience, one state requires a minimum census level to receive payments for bed-holds; however, this policy may vary with individual states. On admission and upon transfer to an acute care setting the bed-hold policy is discussed with the patient. This policy is also communicated to the receiving hospital. If the patient's acute care stay is longer than the bed-hold days, the facility may then extend the bed-hold time for that individual patient as a courtesy. Patients may choose to return to the same facility or request a transfer to different facility of their choice that has a vacancy and meets all their preferences.

Resources

Bartels, S. J., Gill, L., & Naslund, J. A. (2015). The Affordable Care Act, Accountable Care Organizations, and Mental Health Care for Older Adults: Implications and Opportunities. *Harvard Review of Psychiatry, 23*(5), 304–319. http://doi.org/10.1097/HRP.0000000000000086

CMS, (2015), Retrieved from: https://www.cms.gov/Newsroom/MediaReleaseDatabase/Press-releases/2015-Press-releases-items/2015-10-29.html

Elizaitis, B., (2020) Ftag of the week- F560 Right to Refuse Certain Transfers. Retrieved from: https://cmscompliancegroup.com/2020/01/10/ftag-of-the-week-f560-right-to-refuse-certain-transfers/

Ouslander, J. G., Bonner, A., Herndon, L., & Shutes, J. (2014). The INTERACT Quality Improvement Program: An Overview for Medical Directors and Primary Care Clinicians in Long-Term Care. *Journal of the American Medical Director*

Unruh, M. A., Grabowski, D. C., Trivedi, A. N., & Mor, V. (2013). Medicaid Bed-Hold Policies and Hospitalization of Long-Stay Nursing Home Patients. *Health Services Research, 48*(5), 1617–1633.Retrieved from: http://doi.org/10.1111/1475-6773.12054

CHAPTER ELEVEN

Infection Prevention, Hydration and ADL's

Learning Objectives:

Infection prevention is of utmost importance in this setting. Part of patient safety is to prevent the spread of infection. This section elaborates on preventing infections, hydration, and ADL's.

McGeers Criteria

The McGeers criteria was developed for the proper stewardship of antibiotics in the LTC setting and to prevent the development of MDRO's (Stone et al, 2012). The writers also discuss the criteria for determining a true infection, where the determination is not solely based on an isolated lab report for a UTI or a blood infection. Other symptoms must be identified in classifying them as a true infection. The authors of the study by Stone et al. (2012) suggest that one should take note of adequate hydration levels and any potential side effects of medication before deciding a definitive infection. They also recommend including observations of symptoms that are recent and acute, as well as, watching for any mental status changes or sudden changes in vital signs. The IPN is certified and trained to carry out surveillance documentation, including but not limited to monitoring patients on antibiotics, noting symptoms, recording lab and diagnostic results, and evaluating these against McGeers criteria to determine the presence of a genuine infection. The nursing staff should also be trained in recognizing these McGeers criteria and apply monitoring all patients on antibiotic therapies. Not only does the IPN monitor the prevention of infection and see that infections meet McGeers criteria, also, they must also oversee the containment of any infection with precautionary, isolation and quarantine rooms.

Precautionary Rooms

Precautionary rooms are set up primarily to keep infections contained, so that isolated patient with transmittable infections such as a MDRO, are placed in these precautionary rooms. This is especially necessary for a patient with a positive C-Diff infection or positive COVID-19 infection, where the patient is placed in a private room immediately to prevent the spread of the infection to other patients. Personal Protective Equipment (PPE) include items such as gloves, gowns and mask are set up inside the room so that gowning with a PPE can be easily donned and doffed. Receptacles are also set up in the patient's room for clothing items, waste products, gowns, gloves, masks and protective eye wear to be disposed of and where fresh supplies are replenished daily. Another integral component of keeping infections contained is to have staff members and visitors comply with donning the necessary PPE before entering the patient's precautionary room. The increase in growth of MDROs necessitates judicious guarding of the spread of infection. O'Fallon, Pop-Vicas, & D'Agata, (2009) discuss the increase in Multi-Drug Resistant Gram-Negative Organisms (MDRGN), Vancomycin Resistant Enterococcus (VRE) and Methicillin Resistant Staphylococcus Aureus (MRSA), these are just a few of the many organisms to combat and prevent widespread infections. During the annual survey, patients on precautions are observed by the surveyor, specifically noting whether staff or family members are donning the appropriate PPE before entering the patient's room. Information must also be provided on the type of precaution and type of PPE needed while maintaining patient privacy. Methods of infection transmission such as airborne, or droplet precautions, should be specified. This information is made available outside following HIPAA guidelines. The patient's chart is also examined by the surveyor to verify that each care plan reflects the precautionary measures and a physician's order is in the chart that indicates the precautionary status. Patients with infections may have prolonged hospital stays and the goal is to prevent the spread of these infections. Lofgren, (2014) notes, increased mortality with longer inpatient stays in the hospital with C-diff infections; longer hospital stays translate into increased cost in healthcare. Another aspect of keeping infections in check is to perform any therapy in a patient's room with those on specific precautions. The patient should not be allowed to be in any group settings during this time. The IPN monitors patients on precautions and keeps track of patients with these infections. In the past, infected patients were separated in rooms according to their type of infections. However, with an increase in the number of resistant organisms in patients, it is becoming difficult to continue this practice. Always placing patients with active infections in a private room provides an effective means in halting the spread of infection. Keeping infections in check keeps the patient healthy, limits extended stay and is most cost effective.

COVID-19

The Corona Virus- 2019 (COVID-19) became the newest infectious disease challenging the general public, patients and healthcare workers. It became a worldwide pandemic and in a very short time became extremely complex. Initially, there were no treatments available. Several pharmaceutical research companies were working diligently to develop a vaccine that could provide immunity. Eventually, vaccines were finally developed and soon after boosters as well. Early in the spread of the COVID-19 infection throughout the world, it was known to affect the respiratory system and spread primarily through the respiratory system by droplets similar to Tuberculosis (TB) with coughing, talking and sneezing. It was noted that anyone with a compromised immune system or with underlying disease conditions and those with co-morbidities were more vulnerable and more likely to succumb to the deadly virus. The virus was not alive and known to persist on various surfaces for varying periods. The incubation period would last approximately two weeks and a carrier whether exhibiting symptoms or not could infect others. Symptoms were mainly fever, a dry cough and tiredness, others experienced diarrhea and lethargy. An infected person could exhibit flu like symptoms and eventually progress to Acute Respiratory Distress Syndrome (ARDS) and Sepsis leading to multiple organ failures and death.

Positive COVID-19 is detected by swabbing the nose or throat of the suspected patient. Abnormal labs of increased white blood cells (WBC), increased Blood Urea Nitrogen (BUN) and Creatinine (Cr) and abnormal clots forming can develop in these patients, making it extremely challenging to treat. (Guo et al, 2020). Millions of people were infected worldwide while the United States (US) saw tens of thousands of deaths (Worldmeters.info, 2020). Challenges faced by US healthcare workers were staffing, inadequate personal protective equipment (PPE) in the beginning, and later on there were limited amounts of ventilators for the acute care setting. One skilled nursing facility (SNF) on the west coast evacuated patients to an alternate location because staff members did not appear to work for two days in a row (Washington Post,

2020). Patients with droplet precautions are generally managed in a negative air pressure room. Since LTC facilities are not equipped with negative pressure rooms, the suspected COVID-19 patient is usually transferred to a higher level of care specifically acute care treatment. Visitors during the pandemic were required to stay at home and employees who were sick were told not to report to work.

The CDC recommended guidelines to protect each person were specifically to practice social distancing of six feet, good hygiene, avoiding touching facial areas namely the eyes, mouth and face, as well as, covering a cough and a sneeze and halt visitors coming into a LTC center. The environmental department's role became critical to prevent the spread of this infection. All surfaces were to be thoroughly cleaned throughout the day with the appropriate cleaning product (CDC.gov, 2020). Preventing the spread of the infection began with a deep thorough cleaning, proper disposal of soiled disposable outer wear, and a thorough cleaning of a room after a patient is discharged During this time of COVID-19 pandemic, the regular survey was put on hold and a shortened version on the inspection survey was carried out. Facilities were allowed the opportunity to perform their own self-assessment on how they were doing during the heightened time of infections. The management of the LTC center faced numerous challenges, particularly with the surge in the COVID-19 cases and fatalities. Violations at some facilities were complaints of not reporting the COVID-19 infections to family members.

It is required that the facility nursing staff updates family members on each change in condition or health status of the resident. One LTC center was cited for failure to identify and manage ill residents, while some centers failed to notify the department of health. Others were also being cited for failure to have a backup plan. Another LTC center was cited for not providing adequate storage for the deceased, dead bodies were found piled up in a room at the center. CMS has set forth guidelines for testing in facilities where all staff, visitors and residents should be tested. Screening should be done on a daily basis and positive residents should be placed on precautions to prevent the spread of the virus, (WHCA, 2020). As time progressed CMS required facilities to have a Clinical Lab Improvement Amendment (CLIA) such that point of care testing could be performed. Most facilities already have this waiver in place for performing blood glucose testing.

Hydration Status

Vigilant monitoring of each patient's hydration status will reveal a baseline for monitoring potential changes in their condition. It is an indicator of whether adequate fluids have been given or consumed. Hydration monitoring assists in the prevention of re-admissions to the hospital. This achievement comes from a crucial practice to assess baseline hydration status and to observe the early signs of dehydration. Monitoring hydration status should include the following: vital signs, skin turgor, cognition, appearance with any changes in ability to perform normal tasks, recording accurate nutrition and fluid intake at meal times; on all shifts. The nursing staff must report symptoms to the provider and execute a physician's order to prevent any significant decline in health. The charge nurse is responsible for checking the CNA's completed documentation each shift. The nurse must monitor for dehydration and poor PO intake every shift, this involves evaluating the intake amount in milliliter (ml) or ounces (oz) each shift for fluids and amounts in percentages with solid foods. After gathering this data, the nurse then determines if the patient had an inadequate intake of fluids and solids and makes appropriate adjustments with any needed interventions. Each shift the nursing staff is responsible maintaining or improving the patient status by encouraging fluid intake or restricting fluid intake especially for those on fluid restrictions. A dialysis patient, or a Congestive Heart Failure (CHF) patient can potentially develop critical fluid overload and if not managed well can subsequently be transferred to an acute care hospital where it could have been avoided to begin with. Monitoring for inadequate solid intake, or poor fluid intake is critical, carefully considering the patient's health status and activity levels at baseline and always observing for any cognitive decline, dizziness, dry skin and mouth, sunken eyes and constipation. Meticulous monitoring of any non-documentation is vital since this could reflect in the false appearance of the patient's low PO intake, for instance omitting to record actual fluid intake lower than actually consumed. If not identified and addressed early, false low fluid intake can result in reporting to a provider a patient's low fluid intake and orders put in place that were unnecessary. However, true poor fluid intake requires the charge nurse to consult with the provider to obtain orders to correct the issue and consult with the dietician for the critical interventions. Hydration monitoring is nursing 101, this practice is carefully observed during the survey process; where patients are viewed to see if proper support is provided during meals and throughout the day to ensure adequate meal and fluid intake is provided as needed (CMS, 2017). Some patients are unable to express their needs and must be monitored carefully to prevent deterioration or a decline. Therefore, it is highly important to carefully assess for signs and symptoms of dehydration; poor fluid intake can interfere with ADL's and patient recovery.

Activities of Daily Living

Activities of Daily Living (ADL's) is a prime focus in the LTC center especially the late loss ADL's specifically bed mobility, transfers, eating and toilet use; the other ADL's are ambulation, bathing and dressing in this population. Late loss ADL's are ADL'S that are lost later in the course of an illness which manifest with difficulty performing these activities. The target goal of each center is to maintain, improve, or prevent a decrease or loss of each. Diligent effort must be made to prevent loss of bowel or bladder control, prevent reduction in mobility or loss of range of motion. A thorough initial assessment completed helps to determine the performance level and possible interventions that may prevent a decline. The chief purpose for a patient's admission to a STR or LTC rehab is to improve a patient's ability to perform ADL's. For example, a patient with a new incontinent diagnosis should have a toileting plan focused on the times where incontinence is most experienced with periodic assessments to document improvement or decline to make appropriate changes. A patient with an increased need for assistance in these areas require a change in condition completed in the MDS assessment. The MDS documentation captures incidences of late loss ADL's and reports all findings to CMS.

CMS requires a functional assessment on entry to the center and again prior to discharge. Talley et al, (2015) makes mention of the different types of restorative programs supported by Medicare. Each center has the option of focusing on a few ADL's and are reimbursed if the program is administered for at least in 15-minute intervals each time to the resident. A center may choose from the ADL's list and additionally perform assessments regularly to identify patients in need of additional assistance. A patient may require an assistive device for meals, this is determined after an initial assessment, to specifically identify which device such as built-up utensils and plates that best suits the patient to help with independence and prevent a decline with meal portion intake.

To encourage independence in feeding an enhanced dining option may be a focus with speech services involved. Although, the aim is to maintain independence with eating; those patients, in need of additional assistance at meals who are unable to feed themselves, are provided the needed care and assistance. Careful ongoing communication between the MDS department, the Nursing Department and the Rehabilitation Department is very important. Patients with sudden declines in any area must be identified, assessed, and referred appropriately for recommendations and interventions ordered. Obtaining baseline data is significant on an ambulatory patient who may decline after a fall. Nursing identifies these opportunities to make improvements in the patient's level of function and prevent them from worsening by referring early to Occupational Therapy (OT) and Physical Therapy (PT) or Speech Therapy (ST). The Rehabilitation Department works with the patient to improve their physical status and possibly return them to baseline or better. When a change is identified dissemination of information to the nursing staff is significantly important so they can perform their responsibilities accurately and efficiently. Nursing must update the patient's care plans, followed by clear documentation in the nursing notes referencing the problem and interventions put in place to remedy. In addition, the CNA care card is also updated with current changes on the patient's new status. Failure to address a decline in a patient can potentially lead to citations, fines or penalties at the time of the survey; therefore, this should not be ignored and is a major focus by the DON and the nursing team.

Resources

CMS, (2017), Retrieved from:
https://www.cms.gov/regulations-and-guidance/guidance/transmittals/downloads/r36soma.pdf

Guo, Y. R., Cao, Q. D., Hong, Z. S., Tan, Y. Y., Chen, S. D., Jin, H. J., Tan, K. S., Wang, D. Y., & Yan, Y. (2020). The origin, transmission and clinical therapies on coronavirus disease 2019 (COVID-19) outbreak - an update on the status. *Military Medical Research, 7*(1), 11. https://doi.org/10.1186/s40779-020-00240-0

Lofgren, E. T., Cole, S. R., Weber, D. J., Anderson, D. J., & Moehring, R. W. (2014). Hospital-Acquired *Clostridium Difficile Infections Estimating All-Cause Mortality and Length of Stay. Epidemiology (Cambridge, Mass.), 25*(4), 570–575. http://doi.org/10.1097/EDE.0000000000000119

O'Fallon, E., Pop-Vicas, A., & D'Agata, E. (2009). The Emerging Threat of Multidrug-Resistant Gram-Negative Organisms in Long-Term Care Facilities. *The Journals of Gerontology Series A: Biological Sciences and Medical Sciences, 64A*(1), 138–141. http://doi.org/10.1093/gerona/gln020

Stone, N. D., Ashraf, M. S., Calder, J., Crnich, C. J., Crossley, K., Drinka, P. J., ... Bradley, S. F. (2012). Surveillance Definitions of Infections in Long-Term Care Facilities: Revisiting the McGeer Criteria. *Infection Control and Hospital Epidemiology: The Official Journal of the Society of Hospital Epidemiologists of America, 33*(10), 965–977. http://doi.org/10.1086/667743

Washington Post, (2020), Corona virus, wracked nursing home evacuated after most of staff failed to show for two days. Retrieved from: https://www.washingtonpost.com/nation/2020/04/09/california-nursing-home-coronavirus/

WHCA, (2020), CMS Issues New Reporting and
Testing Requirements for Nursing Homes:
Nursing Homes Now Required to Test Staff
and Offer Testing to Residents. Retrieved from:
https://www.whcawical.org/publications/care-
connection/august-28-2020/cms-issues-two-
qso-memos-on-staff-testing-and-clia-
reporting-requirements/

Worldmeter.info, (2020). COVID-19 Coronavirus
Pandemic; Retrieved from:
https://www.worldometers.info/coronavirus/

CHAPTER TWELVE

Staffing Needs

Learning Objectives

One of the challenges for nurse leaders is staffing concerns. Life events do occur on different levels; vacations, childbirth, retirement, sick calls and more. Plans should always be to continuously hire to improve staffing.

Staffing Needs

The everyday nursing function and patient care needs of the center require appropriate staffing levels. In each center the RNs, LPNs, and CNA's are scheduled to care for patient needs on a 24hour basis. The nursing budget is the greater portion of a centers expenditure and to adequately staff a center requires varying hours and schedules with days, evenings, nights and weekends. A combination of 8, 16, 24, 32, and 40 hours per week, including per diem employees and staffing agencies help to facilitate undisturbed patient care. The day shift requires additional staffing for patients to get out of bed, to be toileted, assist with transfer, bathed, transported to all daily therapies, assist with meals, and accompany to outpatient appointments or to attend recreational activities in the center. The evening shift assists patients for meals, transfers, toileting, showers and to return to bed for the night. The night shift requires less staff since patients are sleeping, they will provide toileting and incontinent care needs and prepare patients for early scheduled appointments the next day outside the center. Some companies require staffing based on the census of the facility; if the census is at a certain level, staffing numbers are adjusted accordingly, e.g. lesser staff members are needed if the census is below a set threshold, compared to a census much greater than the minimum level. This type of staffing adjustment does not consider the acuity of patients. A standard form of assuring the appropriate staff levels is to use the patient hour per day (PPD). Tobin, (2009) explains the PPD and emphasizes the importance of compliance and maintaining the appropriate staffing levels. Tobin further describes the F-tag 353, "The facility must have sufficient nursing staff to provide nursing and related services to attain or maintain the highest practicable physical, mental and psycho-social well-being of each patient as determined by patient assessments and individual plan of care." Staff scheduling is accomplished through the efforts of the scheduler and coordination with other nursing team members. The scheduler takes into consideration plans for time off request, including vacation, holiday time off, and illnesses; and immediate call outs for family emergencies that result in staffing shortages for the day. A scheduler's role is demanding, requiring constant precision maintenance and a sharp eye for detail. There are no hard and fast rules for a scheduler but one important proficiency required is to be organized. Kossek et al, (2016) highlight the importance for schedulers in healthcare to maintain compliance with staffing changes. CMS also requires that an RN is on site in the facility at least 8 hours, seven days a week, and that the RN cannot be the DON (CMS, 2013). Nursing is a large portion of the staffing needs in a center and coordination occurs with all departments for a smooth flow, such as the therapy or recreation department. Additional nursing staff is needed for patients who need to be transported to appointments outside the facility. Patients who have early appointments require an early breakfast as appropriate and at times may need an escort if a family member is not available. The physical therapy department may schedule patients for therapy seven days a week and they need to be escorted to the department. One other crucial consideration is the need for a one-to-one sitter for a frequent faller or a patient that is at risk for self-harm.

These circumstances are considered when scheduling the staff for each shift daily. At emergent times, supplemental staffing has to be called in to meet last minute staffing needs. Some healthcare facilities avoid contracting those services and depend solely on their current house staff to fill those vacant slots by them picking up extra shifts or overtime. Procuring such important services are essential in a 24-hour care setting. The state requires appropriate staffing levels, based on the care hours needed for each patient; therapy appointments, assistance with meals, toileting, ambulation, showers and transfers demand adequate staffing. It is essential to coordinate the daily staffing, which requires scrupulous synchronization to provide adequate care and services. A simple call out from a staff member or a mistake in the scheduling for the day result in an extremely stressful day for the staff remaining to provide the same level of care for all the patients if not replaced.

Depending on the LTC center daily operations, a center may hire an RN/LPN that is the Unit Manager (UM) or the Case Manager (CM), Charge Nurses and the CNA's, these roles may be above the required state minimum standards. The state minimum standard has not been adjusted mainly relating to the potential hike in the cost of an already exorbitant level of healthcare costs for the consumer. According to Harrinton et al, (2016), the authors note that the healthcare industry lobbyist has influenced decisions over the years for staffing levels to remain the same, even though, the acuity of patients has increased compared to previous years. The Nursing Home Act of 1987 demanded staffing level improvement but at the time when this was enacted the acuity was to a lesser degree. Sylvestre, et al (2015) describes in detail the importance of consistent staffing based on acuity levels and to also seriously consider other dynamics that contribute to maintaining a consistent nursing workforce. The authors also site mediocre pay, lack of team work, under trained staff, burnout, and poor leadership in maintaining a solid nursing staff. Harrington, Carillo & Garfield, (2017) establishes the position that nursing facilities need to have set minimum staffing levels, although this has been proposed at a higher level, it has not been accomplished effectively. To prevent staffing blunders some facilities take advantage of a Baylor shift scheduling format where individuals work two 12-hour shifts on the weekend, one 8-hour shift during the week, and receives compensation for 40 hours total. This helps to abate staffing concerns, but although innovative, the Baylor shift system may pose problems; in that, replacing a staff member that works the Baylor shift is very difficult on short notice, and so with this in mind, many centers do not utilize this method of staffing. The ideal position to be in for a DON or ADON is to have fully staffed units when overseeing the staffing ratios for compliance. Although some tasks may be delegated, the DON or ADON keeps an open dialogue with supervisors and scheduling staff to make recommendations to prevent such predicaments, in meeting patient care needs. Staffing levels must be reported to Medicare on a quarterly basis; with data including physicians, nursing, contract staffing and any support staff members in each center CMS, (2016). New staffing requirements went into effect Fall 2019, requiring billing to CMS be based on staffing hours. In the past, CMS required billing based on therapy minutes for patient services provided. The new model laid out by CMS now specifies that staffing hours provided for each patient is reported quarterly. (CMS, 2018). Adequate staffing within this new model is very important.

On-Call Rotation

Utilizing an On-Call Rotation (OCR) is extremely necessary to maintain consistent staffing in the event of employee callouts for emergencies and to assist in staffing replacement challenges. It is critical for the DON to set this expectation and solidified in place early in the start of an employee's hiring. An OCR works in favor of the center, with patients and staff members all benefitting. The OCR should be spread out over a year and be scheduled in such a systematic manner that a nurse's rotation on-call is at the minimum. Kikuchi, & Iskil, (2016) discussed the increase in mental and physical distress on a nurse during their on-call rotation. Assuring a nurse is not called in too many times, helps to maintain an employee's well-being. For instance, offering an incentive is quite beneficial and builds employee morale. Each center may set different incentives, where a bonus may be offered for on-call and another incentive for being called in to work. Use of supplemental staffing alone by itself is insufficient to meet the needs. Weekends are notorious for call-outs and preparedness helps to lessen the staffing burden. Inadequate staffing affects patient care therefore, preparing rather than reacting for this potential problem is essential. Although an OCR eases the burden of staffing concerns; it is a small resolution on the greater issue.

Recruiting

Perpetual efforts for recruiting are compulsory, a center cannot defer hiring new staff members until there is a resignation, termination, or retirement creating an opening. A LTC center repeatedly experiences employee turnovers, life events, retirements, promotions, resignations, and terminations. Budget constraints may regulate how frequent and how much can be allocated to hiring new staff members; however, innovative methods, such as, a job fair becomes a formidable approach for attracting a mass selection of recruits. Applications and interviews can commence the same day and selection of candidates occur soon after. Promoting from within is another means of filling open positions and quite advantageous for staff members who are qualified. The prospective applicant is familiar with center operations especially for management positions. An alternative way, though potentially costly, that assists with recruiting efforts is to hire from staffing agencies that have been utilized in the center. Compensation to the agency is customarily required but while the temporary staff is working at the center, direct observation of the worker's performance can be monitored and a determination on whether that temporary staff would be a good fit for the center needs. Another excellent way to recruit reliable, qualified employees are to also offer bonuses for referrals. Staff members will generally refer excellent and qualified people who they are proud to be associated with personally. Recruitment in the long run is advantageous and a necessity. This maintains a funnel of candidates to choose from consistently and prevents an eleventh-hour scurrying, for staff replacement and always being prepared for the inevitable in a successful LTC center.

Assembling the Winning Team

Assembling the winning team commences at the interview process by choosing qualified, motivated, passionate, caring individuals who are desirous of performing well to accomplish the vision and mission of the center. The best option for interviewing new employees is to implement effective means of asking situational questions. From personal experience, situational questions are effective in gathering actual encounters which are potential for future behavior patterns. When used it is quite predictive since the candidate's experience is more likely to be drawn from displaying their own general behaviors or tendency to act. A candidate does not instantaneously assume a new character at a new job; they will perform just as in the past. Selecting a qualified individual is only one part of the battle in operating the day-to-day functions. Assembling the winning team is progressive and requires patience and persistence in developing committed team members. Interviews are the only way to get acquainted with potential candidates from outside the company. As an interviewer, preparation is fundamental; and being unprepared is visible to the prospective candidate when presenting. Prior to meeting with a potential candidate, the interviewer should read through the applicants resume and have questions ready that are circumstantial or open-ended in nature. The interview process can reveal certain things that will assist in deciding to choose the right candidate; for example, tardiness to an interview can reveal historical patterns of appearing to work late. Another example is the type of attire worn that can uncover trends as well. A candidate should be professionally dressed when meeting with their potential employer. It is of significance when someone appears at an interview appropriately attired, frequently this represents how the future employee will appear to the job. In addition, body language such as, slouching in a chair, failure to make eye contact with the interviewer or arms crossed sends negative messages to the interviewer. Body language quickly reveals the interest of the candidate. Slouching may show boredom; no eye contact may reveal noninterest and crossed arms are signs of insecurity or defensiveness. Even though interviews are time consuming and require extensive preparation, it allows for leadership to seek the best employees who will join with the vision of the entire center organization.

Employee Development

Employees who care about their role and the effect on their company tend to seek opportunities for advancement. Employee development prepares and gives each employee the capability to perform their roles in an efficient and safe manner. Employee development is very favorable for a center in several ways. Often, a nursing supervisor could potentially emerge to become the nursing leader as DON which works out to be mutually beneficial both for the organization and the employee. The staff member is already experienced, knowledgeable about the center operation and does not require an extensive orientation to develop in their new role. Promotion from within the organization can occur with new graduates of nursing schools or those who are motivated to aspire to be in a leadership role. A charge nurse could conceivably be promoted to a nursing supervisor and advance even further to perform in the roles of SDC, ADON, IPN or DON. The process of developing each person begins initially with evaluations soon after hire and throughout their tenure as required by the center. This is achieved through monitoring their performance and progression for acceptable standards and completing with a formal performance evaluation, which is generally accomplished after hire at 30, 60, 90 days and then, annually. For state registry purposes there must be an annual review for CNA's, follow up education and documentation of the continued education. Additionally, attendance, tardiness and overall job performance is to be observed consistently. Employee discipline is important and should never be ignored nor should it be a surprise to the employee. Expectations for performance and problems communicated should be addressed timely with the objective in mind to develop the employee into a committed, excellent employee. Supervisors are expected to engage and give input on an employee's performance at each interval of evaluation. Continuing education and in-services assist in increasing knowledge, giving clear direction and effective leadership to the staff.

On-going education in any clinical setting is vitally important, not only, is it important but each person performing their position must be qualified, skilled, knowledgeable and competent. Expertise is measured frequently and can be done randomly to prevent errors and maintain safety for the patients. Patients are to be cared for in a safe manner and competent nursing staff is imperative. On hire, new employees are educated on center policy and procedures for their role, and for performance in the center; including, mandatory education required by the State, the Federal government and Occupation Safety and Health Administration (OSHA). One constant in any center is the certainty of change; both leaders and staff members are kept informed of these continuous changes. Each vacancy may be filled from within the organization and to achieve this, each employee should be growing, learning and developing for the next role. Overall the DON should be perceptive in observing staff members performances that show leadership skills and provide opportunities for promotion internally.

Nursing Competencies

Competencies determine if the nursing staff are skilled and qualified to perform the required tasks. Competencies are verified and documented on hire and on an annual interval basis and made available if state surveyors should request the records. Education compliance involves all the nursing staff, including RNs, LPNs, and CNAs. Training and education must be provided, validated, and recorded, done upon hire, and periodically; thereafter, allowing for demonstration of proficiency. Edelman, (2017) discuss that CNA's show competency in their work performance, as well as, having graduated from a state approved training school with appropriate certification. When retraining is offered the staff member must comply; if there is a refusal to comply with center training requirements, the CNA could be removed from the state registry and prevented from working in this setting in the future.

A center may specialize in treatment of certain patient populations; for instance, Peritoneal Dialyses, Ventilation dependent patients, patients requiring Left Ventricular Assistive Device (LVAD) and Esophagectomy patients. RNs and LPNs should have Intravenous (IV) Certification and Basic Life Support (BLS) training that must also be documented and kept current. It may be more appropriate to contract with an external company for specialized training in a particular nursing specialty, as investing in compliance is of greater importance. An SDC can provide training, but an outside firm may offer more expertise, validate the competencies and provide the certifications. An SDC is also responsible for assuring nurses are competent in medication pass in identifying side effects of meds, contra-indications, ability to administer medications with inhalers, nebulizers and any other form required. Nurses must also show skill in caring for a tracheostomy patient, inserting a Foley catheter, as well as administering medications through a gastrostomy or peg tube. Competency in caring for wounds and assessing and managing them is also a skill that should be monitored frequently. The afore mentioned is not comprehensive but competency is important in the nursing care of patients. Competency can be demonstration through testing or by demonstrating the application of learned skills and knowledge, based on established standards of practice. This is a chance to provide feedback and guidance to the nursing staff. Required training received is then documented for future reference. It is vitally important for the nursing staff to demonstrate competency in all patient care areas; since there is a growing population of chronic ailments in patients admitted to STR and LTC centers. The Institute of Medicine predicted in their book "Retooling for an Aging America: Building the Health Care Workforce in 2008 the growing need for skill in nursing" with geriatric patients. The institute discussed the need for health care workers especially direct care staff to be educated in caring for the complexly ill aging population with multiple co-morbidities today.

Employee Counseling

As a DON/ADON or Supervisor, the center policies must be strictly followed in addressing employee discipline. Employee discipline or counseling opportunities range from tardiness, absence, poor job performance, insubordination, failure to follow policies and procedures, lack of accountability, disregard for authority, and suspected patient abuse. Problems and employee concerns should be addressed timely and should never be an astonishment to the employee. An employee with poor performance in their role may need coaching or may receive additional training to achieve competency. Employee turnover is very costly and to develop an employee into a loyal, efficient, competent individual is considerably more cost effective. Mukamel, (2009) mentions the cost of nurse and CNA turnovers and highlights the potential for other hidden costs of turnovers. Depending upon what a center requires, patience is necessary to see a staff member progress from novice to expert; training and developing the nursing staff helps to retain and keep the costs at minimum for rehiring. Employee counseling done timely is effective in keeping the employee abreast of where they stand and allows opportunities for improvement, growth and development. An initial meeting to address an issue at hand, is an opportunity to communicate expectations and standards for the employee and to see improvement that should be achieved by the next meeting or follow up with the employee. Resolving problems is necessary and should not be ignored or postponed; if the issues are ignored, patient care can be interrupted and employee morale undermined. Discipline should be progressive and after a number of times of counseling an employee should demonstrate progression in improvement. When there is no improvement after many discussions, it may be that the employee does not understand or needs additional education to be deemed proficient. The employee may have no regard for excellence nor desire to improve; this is especially significant for major violations because, patient care and safety is the objective of employee development. As a leader, skill in employee discipline is important and should be developed by the individual. A LTC manager or director must always be prepared for challenges with employee discipline and development, whether employed in an organized union setting or non-union setting. Employee job performance is an ongoing observation process and a DON, ADON, nursing supervisor, charge nurse should always be aware of center operations and proactive in areas where employee growth is needed.

Continuing Education

Continuing education is compulsory. Best practices and constant change require that a nurse keep abreast of current practices. Continual knowledge increase is necessary due to the introduction of new products, medications, laws, regulations, and standards, with current research and evidence-based practices. Qalehsari, Khaghanizadeh, & Ebadi (2017) address the importance of continued education for nurses, they note improved skills and better patient outcomes from additional education. Correa-de-Araujo, (2016) discusses the significance of evidence-based nursing and the positive impact on patient's health outcomes. Upon hire, each person is given a general orientation on the center policies, expected behaviors, standards; center operations, expectations in the role and understanding of their specific job functions. Throughout the tenure of each employee, education is provided on new trends, knowledge for continued practice, changes on legislation and current practice standards.

Each nurse is required to be a graduate of an accredited nursing school in their state of employment. There are different levels of nursing graduates: the diploma nurse, Associate Degree Nurse (ADN), Bachelor of Science in Nursing (BSN), Master of Science (MSN) prepared, and Doctor of Nursing Practice (DNP). Additional education opens up opportunities for career advancement, for example, a nurse may initially be an ADN graduate but advances over time to a DNP. Not only does this open opportunity for career advancement, the patient outcomes weigh heavily on the advanced prepared nurse. Spetz, & Bates (2013) note the demand and need for nurses to be BSN prepared for the advancement in nursing technology. From firsthand experience I have observed eager learners rise to the top because of their willingness to learn new practices, topics and trends in the field of nursing. A willingness to become more educated and skilled, opens doors of opportunities after advancing education is acquired.

Resources

CDC. gov, (2020), Retrieved from:
https://www.cdc.gov/coronavirus/2019-
ncov/community/disinfecting-building-
facility.html

CMS, (2013) CMS Manual, Department of Health and
Human Services. Retrieved from:
https://www.cms.gov/Regulations-and-
Guidance/Guidance/Transmittals/Downloads/
R97SOMA.pdf

CMS, (2017) http://cmscompliancegroup.com/wp-
content/uploads/2017/08/CMS-20062-
Sufficient-and-Competent-Staff.pdf

CMS, (2018)
https://www.cms.gov/Medicare/Quality-
Initiatives-Patient-Assessment-
Instruments/NursingHomeQualityInits/Downl
oads/PBJ-Policy-Manual-Final-V25-11-19-
2018.pdf#:~:text=Mandatory%20submission%
20of%20staffing%20information%20based%2

oon%20payroll,verifiable%20and%20auditable %20data%20in%20a%20uniform%20format

Correa-de-Araujo, R. (2016). Evidence-Based Practice in the United States: Challenges, Progress, and Future Directions. *Health Care for Women International*, 37(1), 2–22. http://doi.org/10.1080/07399332.2015.11022 69

Harrington, C., Carillo, H., & Garfield, R., (2017). Nursing facilities, staffing, patients and facility deficiencies 2009-2015. Retrieved from http://files.kff.org/attachment/REPORT-Nursing-Facilities-Staffing-Patients-and-Facility-Deficiencies-2009-2015

Edelman, T.S. (2017), Staffing requirements: The revised requirements of participation. Retrieved from: https://medicareadvocacy.org/staffing-requirements-the-revised-requirements-of-participation/

Harrington, C., Schnelle, J. F., McGregor, M., & Simmons, S. F. (2016). The Need for Higher Minimum Staffing Standards in U.S. Nursing

Homes. *Health services insights*, 9, 13–19. https://doi.org/10.4137/HSI.S38994

Institute of Medicine (US) Committee on the Future Health Care Workforce for Older Americans. Retooling for an Aging America: Building the Health Care Workforce. Washington (DC): National Academies Press (US); 2008. Available from: https://www.ncbi.nlm.nih.gov/books/NBK215 401/doi: 10.17226/12089

Kikuchi, Y., & Iskil, N. (2016). Influence on sleep and burden on visiting nurses engaged in on-call service during the night. *Epub*, (6) 271-279. Retrieved from: https://www.ncbi.nlm.nih.gov/pubmed/27773 887

Kossek, E. E., Piszczek, M. M., Mcalpine, K. L., Hammer, L. B., & Burke, L. (2016). Filling the Holes: Work Schedulers as Job Crafters of Employment Practice in Long-Term Health Care. *Industrial & Labor Relations Review*,

69(4), 961–990.
http://doi.org/10.1177/0019793916642761

Mukamel, D. B., Spector, W. D., Limcangco, R., Wang, Y., Feng, Z., & Mor, V. (2009). The costs of turnover in nursing homes. *Medical Care, 47*(10), 1039–1045. http://doi.org/10.1097/MLR.0b013e3181a3cc6 2

Qalehsari, M. Q., Khaghanizadeh, M., & Ebadi, A. (2017). Lifelong learning strategies in nursing: A systematic review. *Electronic Physician, 9*(10), 5541–5550. http://doi.org/10.19082/5541

Spetz, J., & Bates, T. (2013). Is a Baccalaureate in Nursing Worth It? The Return to Education, 2000–2008. *Health Services Research, 48*(6 Pt 1), 1859–1878. http://doi.org/10.1111/1475-6773.12104

Sylvestre et al, (2015) Improving the quality of long-term care; Journal of Nursing Regulation, retrieved from: ncsbn.org.

Tobin, P, (2009) Retrieved from: http://tobininsight.blogspot.com/2009/03/long-term-care-how-to-calculate-nursing.html

CHAPTER THIRTEEN

Nursing Administration

Learning Objectives

This section explains and details the function of
the Nursing Administration. Leadership is a must
in any entity and this setting is no different. A
well-managed center is credited to the leadership
in place.

Quality Assurance and Performance Improvement

The Quality Assurance and Performance Improvement (QAPI) at the center level and is one of the initiatives in the new survey process. CMS, (2017) explains the structure for conducting a QAPI program in each center. In years past, Quality Assurance and Performance Improvement were separate, but since the enactment of the ACA, centers are required to set a program in place. The program serves to improve the quality of care and safety among patients while actively involve all the center staff representatives with the consensus and effectiveness of input from the frontline workers. To simply make changes without the input of frontline staff members is ineffective. Areas to improve on vary according to each center and QAPI focuses on maintaining quality standards while assuring compliance with state regulations. Following the state guidelines should be echoed with providing quality care, assure all patient needs are met, and maintaining patient dignity. Applying QAPI principles is a proactive approach, the QAPI system helps to assure patient rights are observed and encourage input from the resident council. Applying QAPI principles identify areas that could potentially be a problem before it escalates into a bigger issue. Improvements are generally after the fact; for instance, when data shows there is an increase in falls or an increase in UTI's, data is analyzed by performing a root cause analysis (RCA) and from there to establish changes for improvement. The Center Administrator oversees this important section, while clinical areas are monitored by the DON/ADON. Implementing QAPI programs will not only look to make improvements but also focus on updating policies and procedures to reflect best practices in nursing and patient care.

Policy and Procedures

Policies and Procedures (P&P) direct patient care in the center, they are made available for all departments. Execution of patient care duties requires clear and concise direction. Every task must follow a P&P and continued education and monitoring should proceed to safeguard that the processes are functioning appropriately. Nursing P&P should be viewed frequently for corrections and adjustments made and updated as necessary. Developing a P&P is an ongoing process with the introduction of new products, process changes, and the general polices on the operation of a center. Newer products are released periodically and regulations are always changing. Reviewing current P&P is imperative to ensure they are not obsolete, and the staff is executing the best practice. The policies should direct safe patient care delivery and be the standard that is followed by all the staff. Flynn, (2011) notes that P&P govern processes of employee actions, center functions and legal aspects.

The challenge for most DONs is to reserve time to accomplish these tasks; whereas, cyclical review will minimize these time constraints. The P&P document primarily emphasizes its title, the objective, and accountable individuals. During the survey process a surveyor doing an inquiry may request a P&P on a matter being explored. If the policy for that issue is not updated, during the annual survey, a center is held to what the policy currently dictates. The center may be practicing with an outdated P&P even though the staff may be carrying out a task correctly. However, if staff members violate the center policy that was not updated during the survey process, such an act may lead to a citation or fine, due to failing to maintain accurate P&P. This makes it vitally important for frequent reviews of the center P&P. After review, the P&P should be approved, with signatures from the administrator, and the nursing leadership team and, also, communicated to the staff. In addition, these documents should be always available for the surveyors if needed.

Annual Survey

Preparing for the annual survey begins immediately after the last survey is completed. This task is a daily process of monitoring every potential area for dysfunction. If a LTC center prepares for survey only in the survey window, the opportunity to correct a system problem that may have occurred over the past year, or eighteen months would have been missed. The survey window opens three months before or after the last survey anniversary and could begin from complaints received from the residents. There are two types of survey; the Traditional Survey and The Quality Indicator Survey (QIS). November 2017 brought changes which are Phase II of the implementation of the new survey process. The new survey process combines the best of both surveys to form one uniformed survey throughout the country. F-tags have been renumbered and there are new items added to the survey process, specifically: Behavioral Health Services, Quality Improvement, Infection Control and monitoring of antibiotic stewardship. There is greater concentration on documentation of admission, discharge, transfers and the patient's rights. Although some centers may have already emphasized a patient centered care, this will now be part of the surveyor's assessment of the quality of care. Facilities are generally required to provide health services such as podiatry, audiology, ophthalmology, and dental. Surveyors now place greater emphasis to observe that patient dentures are replaced by the facility when lost and not at a cost to the patient. There are three parts of the survey process: the initial pool process, the sample selection of patients and the investigative process. The surveyors gather data as they did in the QIS surveys and obtain a sample size based on the facilities census at a maximum of 35 patients. Selection is filtered from admissions, any at-risk patients, complaints, incidents reported and areas identified during the survey. The DON must provide a list of patients with rooms numbered and in alphabetical order, with admissions in the last 30 days. If the center is a smoking facility, the center must provide the list of patients who are smokers along with the smoking policy. The surveyors observe all the daily processes at the center and interview patients, including the activity of each staff members. The interviewing process could extend to as much as eight hours, while past survey interview times took a lot less time. Surveyors also review care areas and meet to discuss any concerns with the resident council leader. All areas of care are generally observed: medication administration by different routes, and the system implemented for storage. The surveyors view and inspect dining activities, infection control practices throughout the facility with surveillance of staff performing duties in precautionary rooms or general handling of patient care activities to prevent the spread of infection. Open and closed records of patients admitted and discharged are also examined by the surveyors. At the end of the survey, if there are any deficiencies, the scope and severity will be differentiated and discussed before the departure; as was traditionally done in the QIS survey (CMS, 2017). The state then issues a 2567 which lists the problems cited, the failure by the facility, the F-tag assigned, with the scope and severity, included. [Fig i]. The center does have the right to dispute a finding if they feel it was unwarranted and that is done through an Informed Dispute Resolution (IDR). Once informed of the deficiencies by the 2567, the nursing leadership develops the plan of correction laying out the actions to correct the deficiencies and the date for completion time. The facility has 60 days to get back into compliance. To be back in compliance means the facility is recertified and is able to accept admissions who have Medicare or Medicaid as a form of payment. On every shift, audits must be completed to show improvement and compliance. When this is achieved the center is placed back into compliance. Prior 2567 were done on paper but more recent submission has been done electronically through the Aspen Web by electronic Plan of Correction (ePOC).

If there are major infractions and continued infringements, this creates a perfect scenario for a state assigned monitor in the facility. A monitor is also known as a Nurse Consultant who overlooks daily processes of all disciplines for compliance and reports back to the state. The Nurse Consultant is available for guidance to the center, but their primary role is obligated to the state. The state is forgiving and gives opportunities for a center to make corrections to comply, but repeated non-compliance and harm to patients may result in the closing of a center. With careful monitoring and correction of compliance concerns consistently, will directly prevent such situations from occurring. These survey results must be made available to the residents and displayed for easy viewing at all times.

CASPER Report

The CASPER is the acronym for Certification and Survey Provider Enhanced Report and is the report card for each center that can be viewed publicly. This access is made available to the management team and allows centers to view their Quality Management (QM) indicators throughout the year and identify areas that need addressing; especially before the annual Health Inspection. The reports focus heavily on skin integrity changes, falls, changes in activities of daily living (ADL's) (CMS, 2019).

F-Tag:

An F-Tag is a number assigned to a problem associated with a deficiency or citation revealed during the annual survey process. Depending on the situation, one F-Tag has the potential to be assigned to multiple problems depending on the category that the problems is categorized under. It is crucial to bear in mind as described in fig 1 that the first level of F-Tags A, B and C may not be serious or no harm to the residents at all.

A level 2 F-Tag is assigned to a problem that is not actual harm but may be an issue or noncompliance with the state regulations. A level 3 F-Tag G, H and I are assigned to incidences of actual harm for instance a pressure injury. A level 4, J, K, and L is assigned to problems that are categorized as Immediate Jeopardy (IJ) to a resident health and safety. In this category monetary fines are assigned in thousands per day. Very important to always keep in mind the Scope of the deficiency, whether it is an isolated incident, a pattern or widespread, including, the number of residents affected or potentially could be affected. An isolated incident means it has only affected a few residents. If a designated pattern is determined, it would mean three or more residents were affected by some system failure in the center. F-Tags will reveal noncompliance, system failures, lack of education, whether policies and policies procedures are followed, or whether it is a persistent problem. It is important to continually have audit tools in place to keep abreast of the center's survey status. This can be accomplished by assessing and analyzing the problem, keeping in mind the potential for harm; avoiding such risks and formulating a plan for correction to the issues analyzed.

	Scope of Deficiency		
Severity of the Deficiency	Isolated	Pattern	Widespread
Immediate Jeopardy to resident health or safety	J	K	L
Actual Harm that is not immediate Jeopardy	G	H	I

Severity of the Deficiency	Scope of Deficiency		
	Isolated	Pattern	Widespread
No Actual Harm with potential for more than minimal harm that is not immediate jeopardy	D	E	F
No Actual Harm with potential for minimal harm	A	B	C

(Fig i)

Five Star Quality Rating

The five-star quality rating as the standard that is widely displayed for the public to view online. (Standards of Care, n.d.) This rating system was enacted in 2008 and is currently exhibited on the website Nursing Home Compare. The areas of focus on the internet site concentrates on the staffing, specifically the number of RN's on staff and the number of RN's working on a daily basis. Patient to nurse ratio and the results of the annual survey from the health inspection are also listed. The online report details any problem observed by the state surveyors, any fines, citations, or deficiencies received by the center during the survey. Short term and long-term care stay patients are referenced in each center report with percentages on ADL declines, patients with pressure ulcers, complaints of pain, falls, and falls with injury, patients with restraints, those with use of catheters, and UTI's (Williams, Straker & Applebaum, 2016). Data for the report card is acquired from the Minimum Data Set (MDS) which is the assessment for each patient submitted to CMS. A high priority for

DONs is directing efforts to decrease the number of falls, systems to prevent pressure ulcer development and UTI's, to assure proper management of pain, and diminish the use of indwelling catheters. Some LTC centers have made strides in becoming a non-restraint center. The 5 -Star rating is reviewed by the nursing leadership on a regular basis to detect areas that need improvement. Although amendments are made and in effect, it takes a while for the results to be reflected on the CMS.gov website. Star equivalency are as follows: 5-Star = Much Above Average; 4 Star = Above Average; 3 Star = Average; 2 Star = Below Average and 1 Star = Much Below Average (CMS, 2017). Every center's goal is to be above average; gaining a 5-star status is an amazing achievement. Diligence with systems in place, careful monitoring, dedicated staff members and commitment by all staff, creates a means to obtain the end goal of a well-run LTC center.

Recreation

The Activities Director in a STC/LTC facility guides the social activities of the center.

Accommodations are generally geared to provide entertainment and appropriate activities for every patient in the center. These activities are personally developed in the resident care plan; each patient coming in the center is assessed for their ability to participate in activities first on admission and periodically throughout the year and while they are admitted to the center. The Activities Department frequently secures the assistances of volunteers, and, at times receive trainees in the particular field. Internship opportunities can provide an excellent experience. Trainees are allowed depending on the center policies. However, the ultimate goal, is to meet the social, and emotional needs of the patients on a daily basis. All patients with a disability, cognitive deficit and even behavioral issues are encouraged to either actively or passively participate in planned activities. A typical day in the life of an Activities Director includes performing assessments on individual patients for the MDS, and also ensuring individual needs are met during group activities or at a one on one individual session. The Activities Director often contracts with outside service musicians to perform sets appropriate for the patients age and era they grew up in and are familiar with. Frequently, themes are planned around holidays accompanied by holiday meals. Common areas such as: the recreation room, large dining areas and other facility areas are used for recreational services. Nursing staff must always observe for opportunities where the patient may benefit from recreational activities every day.

Supplies

Management of center supplies are critical to the function of the Nursing Department. Astute planning and organization help to ensure supplies are always available and to prevent interruption of patient care. Supplies orders and shipment vary in frequency based on the clinical needs and medical conditions. Supplies may be necessary for hourly use throughout the day or used less frequently; but careful monitoring of stock supplies and expiration dates is vital. Very organized personnel are key to keeping a well-run supply department operating efficiently. Supplies may be ordered weekly or biweekly, but the objective is to have a system that meets the needs of each patient and maintain the high regulation standards required by state for compliance. Generally, the supply department is not manned on off shifts; therefore, the center supply coordinator must communicate with the nursing supervisor or housekeeping to assure necessary supplies are available to the nursing units on off shits during the evenings, nights and weekends. Having a supply room organized and labeled will assist in quickly locating items in a short time especially for staff members unfamiliar with the room. Supplies are also part of the nursing budget; consequently, staff should manage supplies to prevent waste. Items such as wound care supplies, creams and soaps can be potentially expensive. Ensuring the provision of quality products meet the needs of each resident is crucial for their well-being. While opting for a reliable brand might come at a higher cost, from personal experience I have seen the difference with a lower quality, less costly wound product and one that was more costly. The more costly product showed better results with quality of care by improving wounds quickly. Having supplies on hand and for quick retrieval enhances care and total wellbeing of each patient.

Resources

CMS, (2017) Nursing Home Compare, Retrieved from: https://www.medicare.gov/NursingHomeCompare/About/nhcinformation.html#main_content

CMS, (2017) QAPI at a glance, Retrieved from: https://www.cms.gov/Medicare/Provider-Enrollment-and-Certification/QAPI/qapiresources.html

CMS, (2019) Casper reporting, Retrieved from: https://qtso.cms.gov/system/files/qtso/cspr_sec13_mds_prvdr_5.pdf

Fig 1, (n.d.) Scope and Severity. Retrieved from: https://www.in.gov/health/reports/QAMIS/ltcr/matrlink.htm

Flynn, N., (2011), Writing effective policies, using written policy to manage behavior, mitigate risks, & maximize compliance. Retrieved from: http://www.epolicyinstitute.com/docs/Prevalent~WritingEffectivePolicy~WPf.pdf

Standards of Care, (nd), 5 Star ratings for nursing homes. Retrieved from: https://www.standardsofcare.org/understanding-care/5-star-ratings-nursing-homes/

Williams, A. Straker, J. K., Applebaum, R. (2016); The Nursing Home Five Star Rating: How Does It Compare to Patient and Family Views of Care? *The Gerontologist*, Volume 56, Retrieved from: https://doi.org/10.1093/geront/gnu043

ABBREVIATIONS

A&I -Accident and Incident

ACA -Affordable Care Act

ACO -Accountable Care Organization

ADL'S -Activities of Daily Living

AND -Associate Degree Nurse

ADON -Assistant Director of Nursing

ANNAC -American Association of Nurse Assessment
Coordination

APM -Alternating Pressure Mattress

APN -Advance Practice Nurse

ARDS -Acute Respiratory Distress Syndrome

BLS -Basic Life Support

BSN -Bachelor of Science in Nursing

BUN -Blood Urea Nitrogen

CASPER -Certification and Survey Provider Enhanced Report

C-Diff -Clostridium Difficile

CHF -Congestive Heart Failure

CLIA -Clinical Lab Improvement Amendment

CM -Case Manager

CMS -Center for Medicare Services

CNA -Certified Nursing Assistant

COVID -19-Coronavirus Disease of 2019

CP -Cardio Pulmonary Resuscitation

Cr -Creatinine

CRC -Clinical Reimbursement Coordinator

DEA -Drug Enforcement Agency

DME -Durable Medical Equipment

DNP -Doctor of Nursing Practice

DON -Director of Nursing

DPH -Department of Public Health

DTI -Deep Tissue Injury

EJA -Elder Justice Act

EMAR -Electronic Medication Administration Record

EMR -Electronic Health Record

EMT -Emergency Medical Technician

EPA -Environmental Protection Agency

ePOC -Electronic Plan of Correction

FTE -Full Time Employee

GI -Gastrointestinal

HC -Homecare

IMPACT -Improving Medicare Post-Acute Care Transformation

IOM -Institute of Medicine

IPN -Infection Prevention Nurse

IV -Intravenous

LAL -Low Air Loss

LNHA -Licensed Nursing Home Administrator

LPN -Licensed Practical Nurse

LRI -Lower Respiratory Infection

LTC -Long Term Care

LVAD -Left Ventricular Assistant Device

LVN -Licensed Vocational Nurse

MAR -Medication Administration Record

MD -Medical Doctor

MDRO -Multi-drug Resistant Organism

MDS -Minimum Data Set

MRN -Medical Record Number

MSN -Master of Science in Nursing

NHRA -Nursing Home Reform Act

NP -Nurse Practitioner

NPWV -Negative Pressure Wound Vac

NSAIDs -Non-steroidal Anti-inflammatory Drugs

OBRA -Omnibus Reconciliation Act

OCR -On Call Rotation

OSHA -Occupational Safety and Health
Administration

OT -Occupational Therapy

OTC -Over the Counter

P&P -Policy & Procedure

PA -Physician's Assistant

PASARR -Pre-admission Screening and Resident Review

PCP -Primary Care Physician

PNA -Pneumonia

PPD -Patient Per Day

PT -Physical Therapy

PTE -Part Time Employee

QAPI -Quality Assurance and Performance Improvement

QIS -Quality Indicator Survey

QM -Quality Management

RCA -Route Cause Analysis

RD -Registered Dietician

RN -Registered Nurse

SDC -Staff Development Coordinator

SNF -Skilled Nursing Facility

SOM -State Operations Manual

STR -Short Term Rehab

TAR -Treatment Administration Record

TB -Tuberculosis

UM -Unit Manager

URI -Upper Respiratory Infection

US -United States

UTI -Urinary Tract Infection

WBC -White Blood Cells

WC -Wound Care Nurse

SUBJECT INDEX

A

Abbreviations, 255

Accident and Incident, 124

Annual Survey, 238

Activities of Daily Living, 196

Admissions department, 23

Alarms, 139

Assembling the Winning Team, 214

Assessments on admission, 55

Assistant Director of Nursing, 22

Audiology Services, 106

B

C

This book has been written with the intention of providing comprehensive guidance on the key aspects of the daily operation of a LTC center. In order to achieve success, having a baseline knowledge is crucial. By reading this book, you will gain valuable insights into all department functions.

It is my hope that the information presented in this book will help you navigate the challenges and complexities of the center operation Success may look different for each individual and I want to offer support and encouragement to all readers in their unique endeavors.

Starting a new role in this arena can be daunting, but the right tools and knowledge can allow you success. Therefore, you are urged to read this book with an open mind and a willingness to learn. Having foreknowledge will equip you with strategies to succeed in a LTC Center.

terry@trinityresource4you.com

Made in the USA
Monee, IL
01 November 2024

69134272R00157